PRAISE FOR
THE GROWN WOMAN'S GUIDE TO ONLINE DATING

"Because I know so many people, I've never seriously considered online dating. But after checking out Margot's book, it might just be in the cards! Not only does she take the guesswork out of it all, but her wit and transparency make the concept so much more inviting. Ladies, I have no doubt you will find it very insightful!"

—Rashad Jennings, former NFL running back and
Dancing with the Stars season 24 champion

"In this social media-saturated world, pursuing a relational connection through a screen can seem silly, superficial, and, to some, unspiritual. In this guide to online dating, Margot puts to rest the taboos that have deterred many women from taking a chance at love. Whether you are new to online dating or have lost hope after years of underwhelming results, Margot navigates this voyage with you and helps you avoid the characteristic setbacks and pitfalls of virtual connection. This guide will give you concrete steps for dating well from the beginning to the end, all while reminding you just how loved you already are."

—Chrystal Evans Hurst, bestselling author and speaker

"With humor, wisdom, and practical answers, Margot speaks not just theoretically, but realistically. There are a ton of dating books in the world, but she narrows the playing field and speaks to problems within dating for grown women. Her heart and voice shine through this book, and I can't wait to send it to my single friends!"

—Bianca Juarez Olthoff, pastor, speaker, and author of the
bestselling *How to Have Your Life Not Suck*

"Margot Starbuck is smart and empowering in her new book *The Grown Woman's Guide to Online Dating*. In a dating landscape that often feels like an endless maze, Margot provides a map for her readers, complete with hard-earned wisdom, fresh insights, and personal anecdotes. She is the girlfriend sitting next to you, the counselor encouraging you, the friend commiserating with you, and, at times, an outlet for the Spirit to guide you. Fire up your phones, prepare your profiles, and realize how lucky you are to have Margot walking through this with you."

—Joy Beth Smith, author of *Party of One: Truth,*
Longing, and the Subtle Art of Singleness

"*The Grown Woman's Guide to Online Dating* is insightful, witty, inspiring, and so very engaging. It's for any woman who wants to successfully navigate the world of online dating by first discovering the unique value she offers to the world."

—Nona Jones, author of *Success from the Inside Out*

"The very day I received Margot Starbuck's new book I tore into it eagerly, reading until midnight. Which is strange since I'm not in the dating market. But I am in the 'good reading' and 'wise and witty' market, which is another way of saying 'I'm in the Margot Starbuck market.' Pass this book on to anyone who's dating or thinking of it. They'll laugh, take notes, avoid tons of awkward dates, and gain buckets of godly savvy. I can't think of a better guide than Starbuck."

—Leslie Leyland Fields, author of *Your Story Matters: Finding,*
Writing, and Living the Truth of Your Life

"As a woman who was divorced and then chose to try online dating, I wish I had had Margot's witty, gentle, honest, soul-helpful advice to guide me on my journey. I would have saved myself some heartache and a lot of time, and would have started the process with the truth: that I am already Beloved as I am. Every dating woman should read this book."

—Elisabeth Klein, author of *Unraveling, Moving On as a Christian Single Mom,*
Dating After Divorce as a Christian Woman, and *Second Time Around*

"Margot Starbuck offers the book equivalent of a long chat over hot cups of coffee, equal parts counsel and commiseration."

— Ruth Buchanan, author of *The Proper Care and Feeding of Singles: How Pastors, Marrieds, and Church Leaders Effectively Support Solo Members*

"This book is so much more than a how-to for online dating! Margot Starbuck serves as your BFF and the most awesome mentor you could ever hope to have. Brimming with rich relational and spiritual insights, *The Grown Woman's Guide to Online Dating* teaches readers to live and love well. It is an indispensable resource for women as they navigate dating in the twenty-first century."

— Dorothy Littell Greco, author of *Making Marriage Beautiful* and *Marriage in the Middle*

"This is a book that meets a screaming need. Finally, *finally*, an insightful, realistic guide to the mysterious world of relationship possibilities that come from dating someone you met online. Margot Starbuck is a voice of wisdom you can trust as you take steps of faith and courage in a new relational venture. I am thrilled to recommend this book!"

— Paula Rinehart, author of *Strong Women, Soft Hearts, And Yet Undaunted,* and *Sex and the Soul of a Woman*

"Margot Starbuck is straight-up hilarious but she's also honest, vulnerable, and deeply insightful. Having been through the world of online dating myself, I wish I'd had a book like this to guide me because it offers practical help combined with sage wisdom. If you are considering getting into this new dating world, are already in it, or just want a great read—buy this book! You won't regret it."

— Vaneetha Risner, author of *Walking Through Fire*

"Let's face it, online dating is tough. Honest, practical, encouraging, and kind, Margot Starbuck is here to walk us through it. Her book will be a guide and a comfort to many women navigating the online dating landscape, pointing out the perils and pitfalls and urging us to stay the course."

— Gina Dalfonzo, author of *One by One: Welcoming the Singles in Your Church*

"*The Grown Woman's Guide to Online Dating* has me just about ready to open my dating apps again to give my profile a refresh. Fun, relatable, and practical, Starbuck walks readers through the all-too-daunting process of putting themselves out there. This book is a must-read for anyone tiptoeing into the world of online dating—especially those who thought they were done with dating for good. Though focused on us single gals, this book is also helpful for the already partnered who want to understand the experiences of their single friends. When it comes to the dating court, Starbuck is the cheerleader we all need."

—Kendall Vanderslice, author of *We Will Feast: Rethinking Dinner, Worship, and the Community of God*

"The dating landscape looks nothing like it did twenty years ago, and for women who grew up hoping a boy would phone on the landline with the long curly telephone cord, this 'swipe right' world can be bewildering. *The Grown Woman's Guide to Online Dating* is anchored in grace and socially savvy in its coaching and cheerleading. Margot Starbuck is the book bestie you'll want to introduce all your girl friends to. She shares everything from top tips for creating a profile to guides to broaching difficult conversations with her characteristic honesty, hilarity, and wisdom. It is possible to remain sane, secure in your identity as God's beloved, and also try online dating: you can trust Margot as a friend and guide."

—Bronwyn Lea, author *Beyond Awkward Side Hugs: Living as Christian Brothers and Sisters in a Sex-Crazed World*

"There is so much to love about this book. It's hilarious, it's practical, it's hopeful, it's wise. But here is what I love most: there are many 'grown women' in our churches who are single and looking for companionship (not just the romantic kind!) and guidance, and Margot lovingly offers herself as both. Her words will no doubt help an oft-overlooked group to feel seen, understood, and dignified, and that's an example we would all do well to follow, no matter our relationship status. I can't wait to share this book with some of the women in my life!"

—Sharon Hodde Miller, author of *Nice: Why We Love to Be Liked and How God Calls Us to More*

the

GROWN WOMAN'S GUIDE

to ONLINE DATING

Lessons Learned While Swiping Right,
Snapping Selfies, and Analyzing Emojis

Margot Starbuck

NELSON
BOOKS

An Imprint of Thomas Nelson

Published in Nashville, Tennessee, by Nelson Books, an imprint of Thomas Nelson. Nelson Books and Thomas Nelson are registered trademarks of HarperCollins Christian Publishing, Inc.

Publishing in association with the literary agency of WordServe Literary Group, Ltd., www.wordserveliterary.com.

Thomas Nelson titles may be purchased in bulk for educational, business, fund-raising, or sales promotional use. For information, please email SpecialMarkets@ThomasNelson.com.

Unless otherwise noted, Scripture quotations are taken from the Holy Bible, New International Version®, NIV®. Copyright © 1973, 1978, 1984, 2011 by Biblica, Inc.® Used by permission of Zondervan. All rights reserved worldwide. www.Zondervan.com. The "NIV" and "New International Version" are trademarks registered in the United States Patent and Trademark Office by Biblica, Inc.®

Scripture quotations marked KJV are from the King James Version. Public domain.

Any Internet addresses, phone numbers, or company or product information printed in this book are offered as a resource and are not intended in any way to be or to imply an endorsement by Thomas Nelson, nor does Thomas Nelson vouch for the existence, content, or services of these sites, phone numbers, companies, or products beyond the life of this book.

ISBN 978-1-4002-1701-4 (eBook)
ISBN 978-1-4002-1700-7 (TP)

Library of Congress Control Number: 2020936467

Printed in the United States of America
20 21 22 23 24   LSC   10 9 8 7 6 5 4 3 2 1

To the beloved women who are dating online—or resisting dating online—I have held you in my heart on every page. My prayer for you is that, amidst a cacophony of competing voices, you will tip your eyes toward the face that delights in you, listen for the voice that cannot lie, and hear it whispering, "You are already the beloved."

To the men I've met on this journey, you've taught me everything. I'm reminded of the Carly Simon lyrics, "You probably think this song is about you." You're not vain at all. This song is absolutely about you. And I secretly hope you read every word.

CONTENTS

CONTENTS

COMMUNICATING WELL

NOTICING WHAT WE BRING TO DATING

SEEKING DISCERNMENT

PRACTICING SELF-CARE WHILE DATING

CONTENTS

WEATHERING THE JOURNEY

NAVIGATING ENDINGS

IMPLEMENTING SIX HEALTHY PRACTICES

INTRODUCTION

What Is Most True

Define yourself radically as
one beloved by God.

—*John Eagan,*
A Traveler Toward the Dawn

Before you date, or while you're dating, I want you to pause to make one important decision. It matters because it's going to impact all the other choices you'll face on the dating journey from here on out: *decide what is most true about who you are.* No one else gets to choose that. Only you do. No matter what comes next, this is the moment to decide that you are, already, entirely beloved. It is the foundational truth to which you can, and should, return often. Make it your own.

You decide if you are a catch who a quality man will be lucky to meet. You decide if you're worth treating well or if you'll put up with a player's games. You decide if you'll settle for whatever guy messages you first or whether you will wait—maybe longer than you might choose—for someone who is emotionally and spiritually equipped to give and receive love.

You are God's beloved.
There's nothing you can do to be more
worthy of love than you already are.
You are accepted, received, and embraced
—in this moment and all others—
by One whose love does not, cannot, fail.
God sees you. God hears you. God
knows you. God loves you.
Nothing can separate you from God's love.
In every moment the voice of Jesus whispers,
"I am the One who is with you and for you."
Now and forever, you are loved beyond all measure.

GETTING STARTED

There's no prerequisites to worthiness. You're born worthy, and I think that's a message a lot of women need to hear.

—*Viola Davis*

one

LAUNCHING

Taking the Plunge into Online Dating

You're not alone.

If you're like me, you didn't wake up one day, look at your life, and think, *The only thing that could make this awesome life any sweeter would be the chance to scroll through my phone, squinting at hundreds of miniature thumbnail photos and tiny-font profiles in search of that needle-in-a-haystack unicorn who is my long-lost soul mate.*

More often, most of us end up considering the possibility of online dating because whatever our "Plan A" was didn't work out.

Our husband died. Or we just never crossed paths with Prince Charming. Or our marriage ended in a divorce we never even saw coming—or maybe we saw it coming for years. Many of us have lived stories that we never would've chosen if we'd been given the choice.

In the first four years after my marriage ended, I was content being single. My heart was healing from the sudden loss of my best friend, I was learning how to be financially independent, and I was focused on the needs of my children. Whenever my Monday morning walking buddy would ask if I'd thought about dating, the answer was always a vehement *no*. I had *no* interest in dating.

Until, one day, I did.

I was at my son's junior varsity soccer game, on the back row of a short stack of bleachers, sitting beside a friend named Bryan, a single man about my age. He'd been dating a great woman, whom he'd met at the local library, for about six months. When Bryan's phone rang, he picked up the call.

"Hey baby," he said affectionately to the caller.

And that was it.

Those two words.

The thought that went through my head in that moment was, *I wouldn't* hate *having somebody call me* baby.

Despite Bryan's success, libraries are not typically hotbeds of budding romance. I had a few friends who'd done online dating and—like most women—I had that one fortunate girlfriend who'd met her amazing husband online. So I decided to give it a try. Like you, I'd heard all the stories: both the ones with fairy-tale endings and the ones that resulted in criminal charges. I didn't know exactly what to expect.

After that soccer game, I went home, stretched out on my chocolaty leather couch, and opened my laptop. I googled eHarmony, typed in my responses to the opening questionnaire, and then typed in my credit card info. Did I breeze through it speedy quick? Yeah, I did. But that's because these sites make signing up ridiculously easy, like they're leaving a trail of bananas in the jungle for a hungry monkey to follow. They *know* that a lot of us aren't tech savvy, and they don't want us to give up and "X" out of their site in frustration. So they design them to be highly user-friendly, with boxes to click and very specific, simple questions to answer (or not answer, if we prefer). Seriously, *monkey bananas.*

As I typed, I was feeling all the feels:

Shame: I would be "seen" and "evaluated" by perfect and imperfect strangers.

Hope: part of me imagined that I'd discover someone awesome on my first day on the site. (I have good karma like that.)

Anxiety: since dating had never ever been my forte, I felt nervous, ruminating on the slim skill set I was offering. I was anxious about engaging in a process over which I felt I had no control.

Entering the world of online dating can feel like venturing through a magical wardrobe into the mysterious land of Narnia. Even if you've heard about this strange world from those who've gone before you, you may still have some trepidation about crossing the portal to the unknown. Or maybe a lot of trepidation.

While my twentysomething and thirtysomething neighbors were generous to give me dating tips, I didn't know any "mature" ladies like myself, approaching our fifth decade, who were in the online dating trenches. No one to suggest the best sites for ladies "of a certain age." No one to advise me about how to attract gentlemen who were as perplexed as I was about whether to swipe left or right. And there was certainly no one to answer the kinds of questions that kept me up at night:

- "Should I believe him when he says he doesn't have any baggage, even though absolutely everyone has baggage?"
- "Should the fact that he describes himself in his profile as 'gun toting' bother me?"
- "Do I tell him about my three amazing children now or later?"

What I needed was a girlfriend next to me as I clicked around online. If this is where you find yourself today, I'm here to be that girlfriend. Though I'm not claiming to be a dating guru—as more than one gentleman I've met online will gladly attest—I have spent enough time in this subculture to have learned a thing or two (definitely more than two). And I'm happy to share some of my hard-won insights in the hopes that they might help you avoid the mistakes I've made and guide you as you navigate your own journey.

Whatever your endgame might be—marriage, companionship, Scrabble buddy—there is richness for you in this season. I know from experience that the dating season is fertile ground for personal and spiritual growth. It's an opportunity for you to trust God to guide you through the foothills and valleys. It's a place to practice following Jesus more closely—because if it's true that discipleship happens wherever you are, then direct messages and meetups are prime places to practice loving God and others.

It also gives you an opportunity to grow as a person, which, I realize, is about as appealing as getting a root canal. It's like what

I've heard my friends who are cancer survivors say when asked to name the best part of having cancer.

Few of us go looking for these kinds of growth opps. And although we can't control the outcome of this adventure, we can—in every moment—choose to trust God and to be transformed by the Holy Spirit into the mighty women we were created to be.

You got this, girl.

two

HESITATIONS

Overcoming Your Fears and Diving In

Today, online dating is a common
way to meet new people.

Many of us who are beginning to date can be bombarded by a chorus of negative voices in our heads attempting to stall us, dissuade us, shame us, and scare us. My own inner voices have lobbed a few of the grenades below, but I've decided that those bullies are not the boss of me. I hope you will too.

"SIGNING UP FOR ONLINE DATING IS TOO DIFFICULT."

If you've ever purchased anything online, you already know that merchants don't want you to get so frustrated by the process that you give up, so they make it as easy as possible to spend your money. Signing up for online dating, which isn't unlike browsing on Amazon, is the same. You'll be guided through the process of setting up an account and creating a profile.

"USING ONLINE DATING SITES IS SHAMEFUL."

As I perused a few men's profiles, I noticed a recurring comment: "I'll lie about how we met." It was my first introduction to the realization that some people feel embarrassed or even ashamed about using dating sites. The suggestion that we hide the fact that we met on a dating app reinforces the shame that Brené Brown identifies as "the fear that we're not good enough."[1] And while online dating once had a sketchy rep back in the early 2000s when it was still fairly new, that's no longer the case. Today it's just a trendy, effective way to meet people.

"ONLINE DATING IS ONLY FOR YOUNG PEOPLE."

While a lot of us are happy to leave hookup sites to the young folks, 49 percent of people over the age of thirty-five have tried online dating![2]

"ONLINE DATING IS EXPENSIVE."

Though some subscription sites *can* cost as much as $60 for a single month, those high rates can be cut by over 80 percent when you choose the twelve-month or twenty-four-month options (great marketing, right?). Some sites are free, but the average customer spends $243 a year, or just over $20 per month.[3] If you're wondering whether the quality of candidates improves on paid sites, I'll make a broad, sweeping generalization and say, "Yes." So if you're willing to join a site like Match or eHarmony, which will cost you, you might have a better initial experience. If you do decide to get your feet wet by trying a free site, then I suggest keeping your expectations low.

"I DON'T THINK I'M READY."

If you are recently single, you might *not* be ready to date. Respect. I've heard the counsel that for every five years you were with a previous partner, you should allow yourself a year to heal after the relationship ends. Although there's clearly no magic formula, that math worked pretty well for me. You honor yourself, and any future partner, by giving yourself the time you deserve to heal emotionally and spiritually. You will know when you're ready.

"MEETING MEN IN PERSON AFTER ONLY CONNECTING WITH THEM ONLINE IS DANGEROUS."

Just as online dating sites want their customers to have an *easy* user experience, they also want them to have a *safe* experience. As a result, you have the opportunity to communicate with men without ever sharing any of your personal contact information. If you make smart choices about the information you share, verify what you learn about him (as much as possible), and are smart about where you finally meet up, the risk is low.

"ONLINE DATING IS A MAJOR TIME COMMITMENT."

Your experience of online dating is going to take as much or as little time as you choose. It will be whatever you make of it. You might go on one date, or no dates, or three hundred dates. It's up to you. If you sign up, explore a bit, and decide it's not for you, you don't owe anyone anything (well, except maybe your credit card company).

"I CAN'T FACE THE REJECTION."

What if a guy doesn't even respond to my message? I've felt enough rejection for one lifetime; why would I go looking for more? Girl, I feel you. You really can't imagine how much I do. And that's why it's important to hold this venture lightly. Approach it with a breezy attitude: "Well, this might be interesting; let's see how it shakes out." When guys didn't respond to my messages, I reminded myself that only 10 percent of messages sent on dating sites get a response. That little mind game really helped me by making it more of a *math* situation than a questioning of my awesomeness.

"DATING ONLINE IS FAILING TO TRUST GOD."

If you're like me, you've asked God to send you that someone special. And some of us have made up the story that the only way to "trust" God with that prayer is to take a hands-off approach and wait quietly for God to send a knight in shining armor to our front doorstep. And while I suppose it's possible that God could send a man riding a white horse into your urban, suburban, or rural neighborhood to sweep you off your feet, I don't think that's the *only* way God answers that prayer. In fact, I believe that God is always inviting us to participate in what he's about. Whether it's our prayers that the poor would be fed or that we'll find a spouse, we are participants in God's kingdom coming on earth as it is in heaven. You can trust God for your future and *also* make an effort to meet someone online.

The reality is that most people I know who do online dating get pretty grumpy about it on the regular. Including me. Any of us who've made an honest attempt to meet someone online often have all kinds of complaints about the sites and the other humans who use them. And yet, IMHO, despite the pitfalls—the dry deserts between matches, the irritations, the constant threat of rejection, and the *actual* rejection—I think it's still a pretty good system. Here's why:

- I can look a guy over without him ever seeing me doing it.
- I kin leurn if he noze how to spel his wurdz.
- I can skim what he's saying about himself to see if he's someone I'd like to get to know better.
- I can discover something about him from the pictures he shares.

As far as I'm concerned, this admittedly imperfect system makes it really easy for me to decide whether I'd like to know more. I'd rather have access to it than not.

My friend Meredith, a savvy therapist, advised, "Think of it only as a means to introduce yourself to folks you wouldn't have met otherwise. You still have to do all the work and investigating." Facts. And because one-fifth of committed relationships today began online, it's still a great way to start.[4]

It's been about twenty-five months since I first signed up for eHarmony. Since then I've been on dates. I've navigated tricky conversations. I've explored other sites. I've been disappointed. I've met a few new friends. I've made mistakes. I've not yet found that special man I'm hoping will call me *baby*. But I've been brave. I've learned about myself. I've grown. And I've even kept a flame of hope that God will provide.

Still waiting.

And trusting that online dating is one tool God might use.

A PERSPECTIVE ON GENDER AND FAITH

When a man says on his profile that he's looking for his "good thing," he's referring to a biblical passage about finding a mate, "Whoso findeth a wife findeth a good thing, and obtaineth favour of the Lord" (Prov. 18:22 KJV). In some Christian traditions, which have possibly been tangled up with centuries of patriarchy, this means—quite literally—that the man does the finding and the woman gets found. One woman cited this verse from Proverbs in her online profile and announced, "If I'm searching, I'm technically out of order. So I'm simply positioning myself to be found." Respect, sister. And while she and I might disagree on exactly how much agency she has in this matrimonial game of hide-and-seek, I do applaud her for putting her profile online. She's been intentional about making herself available to be found. If you've been raised in a wait-and-get-found tradition, it's worth noticing and deciding how you participate, or don't partici-pate, in God's good will for you.

CRAFTING YOUR PROFILE

Our deepest fear is not that we are inadequate. Our deepest fear is that we are powerful beyond measure. . . . We ask ourselves, Who am I to be brilliant, gorgeous, talented, fabulous? Actually, who are you *not* to be? . . . We were born to make manifest the glory of God that is within us. . . . And as we let our own light shine, we unconsciously give other people permission to do the same.

—*Marianne Williamson*

three

SAY SOMETHING
ONLY YOU CAN SAY

Going Beyond "I Love Eating Out"

When your profile says what every other woman
is saying, you don't stand out from the crowd.

When I coach kids who are writing college application essays, I beg them not to write about the time their sports team won the state championship, or when they failed the big test, or when their dog died, or when their life was forever changed because they went on a seven-day mission trip and met a person who was happy despite being financially poor. What these students don't realize is that all the folks, at all the colleges, reading all the essays, have already seen a bazillion essays about the game, the test, the dog, and the happy person. So I coach each of these high school students to write an essay that no one else could write. It's what I want you to do for your profile too. Don't say what hundreds of other women are also saying.

One funny guy—who'd clearly read lots of women's profiles—began his by saying, "I think we can all agree that we all love the beach." That made me laugh. It's funny because he's acknowledging that lots of us women gush about how we love the beach. Write something that no other woman *but you* could write.

As I scrolled through thousands of *men's* profiles, I began to notice that many of those sounded similar too. I noticed popular genres of pictures: "selfie behind the steering wheel," "shirtless at the gym," "me wearing my baseball cap backward," and "I caught a big fish."

So, naturally, I wondered, *What do men see when they scroll through thousands of women's profiles?* I was pretty sure I wasn't going to find "shirtless at the gym," but otherwise, I didn't know what to expect. Since I only had access to men's profiles—that's the way these sites set up their matchmaking—I decided to make a fake dude profile.

I didn't want any *real women* wasting one moment of time on this imaginary guy—whose screen name was "ImJustLookingOnline"—so I made him as nondescript as possible: he was your basic forty-nine-year-old, five-foot-ten white dude whose profession was "management." *Super* vanilla. Mr. ImJustLookingOnline had only eight words to say about himself:

Not sure why im here maybe just lookin

Because I was so committed to making this guy as unappealing to women as possible, I put an inordinate amount of thought into those eight words. I kept this profile just long enough to scope out the profiles of twenty women, of various ethnicities, who shared most of my other demographic info: age, education, kids, etc. Then I deleted the profile and no one was the wiser.

Except you and me.

And here's what I learned about us gals:

LIKE MEN, WE LOVE THE BATHROOM MIRROR SELFIE.

Yes, the bathroom mirror is often the best mirror in the house. Yes, it lets us show off even more of the amazing outfit we labored mightily to put together—even though we want to appear as if we just look awesome all the time, with little effort. But we can do better, ladies. Ask a friend or neighbor to snap a few shots of you outside. Or consider using a timer on your camera phone so you can stand in front of something interesting. Be better.

LIKE MEN, WE CAN TAKE OURSELVES A LITTLE TOO SERIOUSLY.

Maybe we've all watched too many episodes of *America's Next Top Model* or the goofy Ben Stiller movie about male models called *Zoolander*. We're staring into the camera, taking our arm's-reach selfies, and our faces are void of any human expression whatso-ever. I get that choosing photos of yourself isn't easy, but I believe that a warm, welcoming face is more inviting than a closed, cool, way-too-serious face.

LIKE MEN, WE'RE PRONE TO SHARE HUMBLE FITNESS BRAGS.

Because I'd read about so many men's fitness regimes on their profiles, I assumed that it was a "guy thing" to announce how often a man works out at the gym. (*Whatever. Meathead.*) But as I scrolled through women's profiles, I saw that women also loved letting the gentlemen know the ways they were staying in shape. And just as I was silently judging them, I stumbled across my own profile and was reminded of my walking, skating, and swimming regime. Heart check.

LIKE MEN, WE'RE PROUD OF OUR ADAPTABILITY.

Like the guys who brag about working out and then cleaning up for a night on the town, we like to brag about our versatility. "I love getting dressed up for a candlelit dinner, but I can also throw on a baseball cap and go to McDonalds." "I can wear heels to the symphony and come home and watch Netflix in sweats." We really like to let others know that we will not be limited to any single recreational activity or fashion choice.

LIKE MEN, WE DON'T LIKE TO PLAY GAMES.

Lots of men's profiles announced that they didn't want to "play games." Naturally, I was dying to know what these *games* were. After asking both men and women, I learned a few of them:

- Showing up late
- Flirting with the waitress
- Suddenly leaving a date without an explanation
- "Forgetting" one's wallet
- Saying you had a great time when you're not the least bit interested in another date
- Saying you'll call when you have no intention of calling
- Avoiding or not responding to text messages

Now I see why no one wants to play. They're the worst games ever.

MORE THAN MEN, WE LIKE TO FEATURE OUR RELATIONSHIPS WITH OUR PETS.

Perusing women's profiles, I saw a lot of photos of women on the couch with four-legged friends. (I presume that's like tacitly saying, "See?! Animals love me. You will too.")

LIKE SOME MEN, WE LIKE TO ANNOUNCE WE'RE NOT LOOKING FOR A HOOKUP.

Some guys will clearly state that they're not looking for a hookup. Apparently women say it, too, because one frustrated gentleman remarked, "Everybody knows you're not looking for a hookup . . . could you all stop saying that?"

SOMEWHAT LIKE MEN, WE LIKE TO SHARE OUR CLEAVAGE.

The female equivalent of the male shirtless, bicep-flexing gym selfie is the boob shot. If we're wearing low-cut shirts, a lot of us like to hold the camera up high, or extend it out in front of us, to highlight our cleavage.

LIKE MEN, WE LIKE TO TROT OUT A NUMBER OF COMMON REFRAINS IN THE NARRATIVE SECTION OF OUR PROFILES.

These worn-out expressions and tired tropes are not helping us stand out, ladies. While it's unlikely that repeating any of these tired lines will necessarily be a deal-breaker, they also don't distinguish us from the thousands of other women who've said exactly the same things. Examples are:

- I'm looking for a partner in crime.
- I'm not looking for someone who's perfect, but someone who's perfect for me.
- I'm looking for someone I can't live without.
- I won't settle.
- I don't need drama.
- I don't need your money, I have my own.
- I love being happy.
- I like eating out.
- I view the glass as half full.
- I never met a stranger.
- I am comfortable in my skin.
- I'm not perfect.
- I enjoy outings but also enjoy spending time at home.
- I love all types of music except rap.
- I stay in shape by going to the gym.
- I'm a sister, a mother, an aunt, a daughter.
- I love spending time with friends.
- Nobody reads these profiles.

If there's something listed above that's really *important* for you to say, you could write it into your profile in a way that's uniquely your own. For instance, if I wanted to say, "Nobody reads these profiles" (which I wouldn't), I'd instead playfully offer something like, "If you read all these words, you deserve a grape Popsicle. My treat." I'd still be saying "nobody reads these profiles," but in a way that's memorable about me.

The reason I'm so passionate about you articulating what makes you different from every other woman is because you *are* different from every other woman. Remember: what you share about yourself is an on-ramp for a man to discover more about you. Keep reading to discover what *not* to do—and what you can easily do—to reveal what's special and unique about you.

four

DON'T SAY *NOTHING*

Show a Reader Who You Really Are

When you reveal who you really are, you shine.

As you consider what to include in your profile, I am absolutely delighted to share with you the worst profile ever written in the history of the world. It's fictional, but it's based on examples from 100 percent real profiles. Let me be clear: It's not a profile of the worst *human* in the world. I have no interest in throwing anyone under the bus. In fact, the writer represented by this profile might be a stellar human being. Short of being a psychic or hiring a private detective, though, there'd just be no way to *discern* much about the person behind the profile because the profile fails to reveal what is unique about the writer. I want to share it so you can learn what to avoid when you're writing your own.

My Story

We all have a story at this age.

About You

What you see is what you get. I'm just me.

Job

I got one.

What are you doing with your life?

I am trying to enjoy life.

Your Hobbies

Ask me.

Your Favorite Books

I do read books but not gonna get up to find the names.

Your Favorite Food

I like to eat any food that is good.

How You Spend Your Free Time

Sleep.

I'm really good at

Everything I put my mind to.

6 things I could never live without

Myself, air, light, food, water, sunlight.

I spend a lot of time thinking about
There are so many things to think about so I spend a little time on each one.

About what are you passionate?
I work a lot so I don't have a lot of free time.

A typical Friday night I am
Hopefully doing something I enjoy.

About the one I'm looking for
I will know her when I meet her.

What's one thing most people don't know about you?
I tend to get bored easy.

Anything more you'd like people to know
I'm not going to put too much about me because then we would have nothing to talk about.

You should message me if
You want to get to know me.

"Margot," you may protest, "that profile can't be real."
It can't?
Cut and paste, people.
Cut. And. Paste.
Every time a guy wrote that he couldn't live without "air," I wanted to bludgeon him. An overreaction? Probably. But he'd wasted the opportunity to reveal a glimpse of who he was.

He could have gone with, "I can't live without my golden doodle."

Or, "I can't live without Dr. Scholl's inserts in my soccer cleats."

Heck, even "I can't live without Doritos" is better than "air."

Am I a snooty writing snob?

Absolutely. Guilty as charged.

Do I expect every Paul, Dave, and Barry out there to be eloquent writers? Not at all. Of course not. You don't have to be a writing savant to craft a great profile. The most important thing you can communicate in a profile is what makes you the unique person you are.

WRITING A DISTINCTIVE PROFILE

As you write your profile, identify what makes you who you are. Reveal what's special about you. Describe how you are different from other women. I'm not saying that you need to swallow fire, jump out of airplanes, or twerk on weekends as a backup dancer for Beyoncé. (Although, if any of those are you, awesome. Definitely mention those in your profile.) I'm saying that whatever it is about you that is unique—advocating for endangered forest rodents, curating a miniature snow-globe collection, owning a life-size cutout of Michael Jordan—is what will engage the imaginations of others and make your profile memorable.

- Instead of "I volunteer on Saturdays," try, "This week I got to walk a huge Dalmatian at the animal shelter."

- Instead of "I'm creative," try, "I paint miniature watercolors of flowers from neighbors' gardens."
- Instead of "I stay in shape," try, "Saturday mornings you'll find me cycling on the Prairie Path."
- Instead of "I love crafts," try, "Last Halloween I made this mammoth pumpkin piñata that was five feet wide."
- Instead of "I like cooking," try, "My cinnamon apple pie won runner-up at last year's state fair. Just sayin'."

In any writing pursuit, being specific is more interesting to readers than being vague.

I suspect that at some point you've thought to yourself, *So, Miss Margot Smartie Pants, what did you write on your profile?* Well, it's not genius, but my friends have confirmed that it captures who I am:

I love love love my work as a collaborative writer, helping others tell their amazing stories. Seriously, best job ever. (Athletes, entertainers, overcomers . . .) I'm grateful for my beautiful community (ask me!) & I have a lot of energy for life. I love being active outside for a few hours each day—walking, skating, swimming. Have I done standup? Yeah . . . I have. Was I recently recruited to do roller derby? Also yes. (Still deliberating this one . . . because not being injured is also one of my favorite things.) I try to love folks on the world's margins the way Jesus did. Wall of heroes in our kitchen includes Jesus, MLK Jr., Oscar Romero, Bree Newsome, and Colin Kaepernick. I'm looking for character and for someone who's giving back. And he'll be a man of faith.

EDITING YOUR PROFILE AFTER WRITING IT

Now, I don't expect to win any literary prizes for my janky little paragraph, but it does express something of who I am.

I'm both a writer and an editor, but I still find it challenging to write about myself and to edit my own stuff. So after you write your profile, I want you to copy it and paste it into an email to a few of your girlfriends and ask for their opinions.

Feedback from friends is really important because they already know what is charming and winsome and captivating and rare about you. Trust them. And when you return to edit your profile with their feedback, remember that "showing" is always better than "telling." Don't just *say* that your friends think you're hilarious. Give specific examples. Maybe you describe the time you were selected to attempt a half-court shot at a Lakers game and landed on your backside. Or the time you were brought up onstage at *The Tonight Show with Jimmy Fallon*. Or about your near-drowning episode after being forced to go white-water rafting. Let the reader *see* who you are.

Bottom line, there is no one like you in all the world. This is a fact. So show what it is that makes you different from your college roommate, or your neighbor, or your sister-in-law. When you are able to communicate what it is that makes you unique, you give a gift to the person who gets to discover who God has made you to be.

You can also discover and implement eight proven practices that will help you stand out from the crowd!

I DID IT SO YOU DON'T HAVE TO

"I Joined Sixteen Dating Sites"

Did I join sixteen sites because I wanted to gather as much information to share with you, my reading friend, as I could? Yes, I did. Did I sort of secretly hope that Mr. Right would magically be on that sixteenth site? Possibly. But keeping up with all the alerts and winks and messages gobbled up time and was also pretty taxing emotionally. I do *not* recommend it! But there are over 7,500 dating sites on this planet. I thought sixteen felt pretty conservative at the time.[1] As I toggled between them, I could see men who were also on a number of sites—whom, I confess, I silently judged, since what are the odds they were also writing a book about online dating?—so I know I wasn't alone. You'll do fine on one or two sites.

five

SHINE

8 Tips for Crafting an Irresistible Profile

You can create a winning dating profile.

When I came across a profile of a guy whose screen name was "GonnaMakeYouSmile," I was equally intrigued and confused. He wasn't smiling in any of the photos he'd posted of himself. Seriously, I couldn't tell if he even had teeth. Those morose selfies made me distrust his audacious claim to be able to make me smile, and there's a good reason I was suspicious: what we're *shown* is more compelling than what we're *told*.

If you're a reader of memoirs, think of the ones that have been hard for you to put down, the ones that keep you reading way past your bedtime. You promised yourself you'd turn off the light after you finished the chapter, but then you kept turning the pages. Aren't online profiles just mini memoirs? The best ones share one critical quality that's the mark of good writing: *show, don't tell.*

If a man *says* his kids mean the world to him, you're left wondering what that means exactly. But if he describes the scramble of packing grapes and sunscreen for his kids' three Saturday morning soccer games, you can see it for yourself. If he *tells* you he thinks he's hysterically funny (*ick*) but there's no evidence to back it up, do you believe him? But if he writes, "I love online dating. Said no one. Ever," then you at least know he's sort of a witty guy. If a man tells you that he has close friends *and* he posts a photo of him with those buddies while they're spending a weekend at a Habitat for Humanity build, you're going to want to lock that bad boy down. The best way to create a compelling profile is *show, don't tell.*

When you show and don't tell, you're offering a reader specific *evidence* to prove what you're saying is true. This is why I want your profile to read like a bestselling memoir. *Kidding.* As you draft your profile, I simply want you to *describe* what you're saying. You can do this. While you'll eventually need to paste it into the online form, I want you to create your first draft in a separate document so you can run it past your buddies and edit it after their feedback.

Here are my eight tips for making your profile irresistible.

1. CHOOSE A GOOD SCREEN NAME.

I could sort of understand what men were thinking when they chose screen names like MarkSmith68, ProudArmyVet, PeaceDude, or HarleyRider4Ever. I get it. But I had more trouble understanding exactly what gentlemen were hoping to communicate by choosing screen names like "Tired1," "Clueless1," "IWantUrBody," or "LoveSucks27."

Screen names matter to some women. So put a little effort into the one by which you'll be known. Are you RockyRoadForLife?

MonopolyChamp? TennisTeamCaptain? GardeningGoddess? RoadTripWithMe? Your screen name signals something about who you are. Make it count.

2. SHARE PICTURES THAT ALLOW YOUR UNIQUENESS TO SHINE.

I'd love to assure you that, when it comes to online dating, it's what's on the inside that counts. That appearances don't matter. That no one looks at the pictures. But, of course, I can't in good conscience do that. The pictures you choose to post on your profile do matter. (More on this in the next chapter!)

3. CRAFT A PROFILE THAT HIGHLIGHTS WHAT MAKES YOU UNIQUELY *YOU*.

If it hasn't sunk in yet, I'll say it again: I am desperately begging you to craft a profile that no one else on the planet could post besides you. That's the big profile win, friend!

4. OFFER JUST THE RIGHT AMOUNT OF INFORMATION.

When it comes to your online profile, you don't want to write too *little*, and you don't want to write too *much*. It's a classic Goldilocks and the Three Bears situation: you want to share an amount of information that is *just right*.

> **Don't write too little.** If your entire profile reads, "I'm here, world, check me out," a visitor learns nothing about you. You have literally said nothing more than "I exist."

Which is not as compelling as you might think. A number of men's profiles I read said something along the lines of, "Just ask me." Nope. You need to share more than that if you want to interest a guy.

Don't write too much. If you ramble on with too many words, readers will stop reading. While you may feel obligated to share your thoughts on blind dates, global warming, people who post pictures of their salads on Instagram, men who drive monster trucks, why you're obsessed with kitten memes, and how your sister is the real beauty in the family, most people just don't want to know that much information about you until they know you better. They might also bail because it simply takes too much time and energy to read it all (and being random can be a red flag for some people). Keep it simple. Sharing two paragraphs about yourself is a good amount.

5. COMMUNICATE WHAT IS POSITIVE, NOT NEGATIVE.

Sometimes I'll read a profile where the user *wastes* his valuable online real estate by announcing that he doesn't want to be with anyone who's hung up on their ex. Or he'll complain about women who only say "Hi" when they message. Or he'll grump about women who *don't* say "Hi" when they message. Or he'll whine about women who "ghost," which means they disappear without warning by simply disengaging without explanation. Or he'll insist that all women only want texting buddies. And that's all just in the "Say Something About Yourself" section. Negativity detracts rather than attracts.

The kind of profiles that others want to engage with are those that are kind, or playful, or witty, or winsome, or generous, or affirming, or creative, or unique, or inspiring, or clever. You don't need to *be* all those things, but you do need to offer something that people will enjoy reading. Be positive. Name what makes you laugh. Describe your perfect day. Share your favorite shape of pasta. Reveal your favorite superhero. Give someone the opportunity to see the positive side of what makes you *you*. Now, that's attractive!

6. PUT YOUR BEST FOOT FORWARD.

In the fabulous movie *Hitch*, Will Smith plays a New York City date doctor named Hitch who helps men meet and date awesome women. He advises men to strike the delicate balance between letting it all hang out, in the ugliest kind of way, and putting on a pretty mask, pretending to be someone you're not. He explains, "She may not want the whole truth, but she does want the real you. She may not want to see it all at once, but she does want to see it."[1] What I took away from that was, "Put your best foot forward."

This makes me think of the results from my "chemistry test" on a dating site called Plenty of Fish. I answered a bunch of questions and then received my results. In my first quick skim, I zeroed in on flattering phrases like "With the strong degree of self-confidence you possess," and "You likely get along with most people quite well." At that point, I decided that it was clearly an accurate, scientific test.

But then things went south about halfway through the report where I read, "In situations where it is necessary to be focused and careful, you might find that you do or say things that may be inappropriate. As someone who exerts little control over your actions, you may find that you commit social blunders that might offend other people and get yourself in trouble." So, obviously, I changed my mind and decided the test was a sham full of bogus feedback.

My opinion of those results aside, what I learned from that assessment was exactly what Hitch was hinting at. Eventually I'll share *all* of who I am with someone, including my tendency for inappropriate blurting, but until a relationship is pretty solid, it's not the worst idea for me to consider using some filters.

7. REVEAL YOUR CHARACTER.

Quality men will be looking for some signs that you are a woman of character and depth. If you only talk about going to the beach and buying new shoes at Nordstrom's, or sipping margaritas and watching *Keeping Up with the Kardashians*, you're likely presenting yourself as a person who lacks depth. Do you have a favorite author? Are you passionate about a cause? Do you mentor young single moms? Did you learn Greek to study the Scriptures? Give others a chance to not only see that you're fun and playful but also see that you are a woman of substance.

8. BE CONFIDENT.

If you think you're awesome, others will also. If you don't mention what makes you special, then others don't have any way of knowing. Don't be afraid to let your strengths shine without bragging or boasting.

The very best profile you can craft is the one that gives a man the opportunity to notice what makes you *you*. And the pictures you choose are also going to help him see *you*.

six

"SAY CHEESE!"

Because Each Picture Really Is Worth a Thousand Words

The best pictures to include in your profile are
ones that help a man know who you are.

Like it or not, the pictures you post on your profile matter.

For some of us, that feels like the bad news.

But the good news is that you don't have to look like a super-model to create an attractive profile that communicates who you are.

You're entirely unique in all the world, and photos are a great way to demonstrate that. The best profile photos are the ones that show what makes you *different* from the thousands of other women out there. So be thoughtful about how you can communicate the uniqueness of who you are with the photos you choose.

Use these best practices when posting photos to your profile.

USE QUALITY PICTURES.

Invite a friend to take a few good shots of you. If you have a photographer friend with a real camera, ask that person. Or just use or borrow an iPhone that has portrait mode. Snapping pictures outdoors, with the sun behind the photographer, is the best way to get great lighting. Days with a little cloud cover will diffuse the light and make better photos than when the blinding light shines right in your eyes. If you simply must include a mirror selfie because you looked so stunning the night of the big gala that you attended solo (you go, girl!), at least try to devise a way to take it without showing your cell phone in the picture.

SHOW YOUR FACE.

Use a high-quality photo, taken in good light, without anyone else in the picture, for your profile photo. (While it's obvious to you and your mom which person you are, the men skimming through profiles are forced to guess which woman you are.)

SHOW ALL OF YOU.

Be sure to include at least one shot that shows your whole body. Modest, of course. Keep in mind that both the cleavage shot and the downward-facing dog are cliché profile photos that even men say they are tired of seeing (well, probably not *all* men . . . but probably the men I would want to consider dating).

POST A VARIETY OF PHOTOS.

Posting eight near-identical selfies taken behind the wheel of your car while wearing different tops doesn't show a very broad range of who you are. Posting a diverse collection of pictures, headshots and full-body, alone and with others, in a variety of settings, communicates more of who you are. Share pictures from work, or play, or church, or volunteering. Share pictures that include friends, or family, or neighbors. Share pictures of you doing the things you love: playing Yahtzee, or picking strawberries, or throwing a clay pot. Your pictures give someone an extra glimpse into what makes you uniquely *you*.

POST CURRENT PHOTOS.

Research shows that 20 percent of women admit to posting pictures of when they were younger and thinner.[1] At my age that also means firmer, less gray, and less pasty. Between you and me, I think the real number of women who've scavenged for pictures that we think make us look a wee bit better than we actually do right now has got to be *much* higher. (Because I've been inside my own head, I know.) I want you to post current photos for two reasons:

1. Post current photos for *you*. By posting old pictures where you supposedly look "better," the subtle message to which you're agreeing is that you're not good enough, now, *as you are*. Which isn't true. You confirm what's most true when you agree that who you are is good enough and post current photos. (I can hear how "good enough" may

sound like a pretty low bar. But the bar in our culture is too high and too distorted, IMO. You *are* enough!)

2. Post current photos for *him*. On a few different dates, guys have reported to me their experiences of showing up for dates and meeting women who looked nothing like their photos. And you know what? They felt deceived. (And they'd been robbed of the chance to *not* be superficial!) Regardless of our age or size or firmness or coloring, men deserve better. It's not a strong start to any relationship. Post current photos to be fair to *men* who are earnestly looking for a woman to date.

CONSIDER WHAT YOUR IMAGE MIGHT BE QUIETLY COMMUNICATING.

Be thoughtful about what your photograph is communicating to viewers who don't yet know all of who you are. Right now, on my phone, one picture includes a theologically conservative magazine article I wrote for teens, and one shows me wearing my Black Lives Matter T-shirt. Because one picture could ostracize half of the men I genuinely want to meet, and the other picture could likely ostracize the other half, I will include neither of those photos in my profile, even though both do signal an authentic part of who I am.

SMILE!

After scrolling through hundreds of millions of profiles of men and women, it becomes clear that not everyone realizes what a win a smile can be. A warm, engaging face communicates that you are a warm, engaging person. A cool, closed face communicates distance. That said, not every picture needs to include smiles that show every last one of your teeth. I confess, I made this mistake. When a girlfriend noticed that each of my photos featured a decidedly manic grin, she asked a friend we were with at the time to take a few less smiley photos of me. My profile is better for it.

Now that you've gotten your poop in a group, having put together a strong profile, you get to start checking out men's profiles. It's about to get real, girl.

BE UNIQUELY YOU!

Avoid these overused types of photos that make you blend in instead of stand out.

- Duck lips
- Snapchat face recognition filters with animal noses and ears
- Cleavage shots
- Booty shots
- Lingerie
- Twenty pictures from the neck up that look nearly identical
- Too many pictures with more than one person

BROWSING MEN'S PROFILES

Listen to what a man says, watch what he does.

—*A. H. Carlisle*

seven

A MAN'S LOOKS

Though It's Not All About Appearances, Some of It Is

Instead of pretending that appearances
mean nothing, admit that they mean
something and seek God's vision.

I usually scroll past men's profiles that are shouty, which means WRITTEN IN ALL CAPS. And I also pass by ones where a dude clearly has an ax to grind with all women, everywhere. And yet somehow, I got drawn into one of these "ax to grind" profiles last night. And as I read this gentleman's profile, and realized what he was doing, I couldn't stop reading. Because he had successfully executed a freakin' *sting operation* on Match.com.

Who is this mystery man, you ask? I don't know. For our purposes, I'll call him Sting.

Sting began a bit aggressively, "OK LETS BE REAL HERE . . . IT IS ABOUT LOOKS!"

Although shouty, he'd captured my attention.

Sting then went on to say he was a good man with a good résumé. For the sake of this discussion we'll just take his word on that. Sting said he'd reached out to a number of women over the three months he'd been on Match.com and received only four replies. In other words, the majority of women Sting messaged did not reply.

As I read, I discovered that Sting believed that women weren't responding to his messages based on his appearance. And while I don't know what Sting looks like—and you're about to find out why—I'm going to assume that he's not that classic Robert Redford, Denzel Washington, Benjamin Bratt kind of handsome. For whatever reason—an odd-shaped nose, or pasty pale skin, or hair in all the wrong places, or carrying a few extra pounds— Sting was convinced that women weren't responding to his messages because of how he looks.

And that's when he put his genius plan into action.

Sting revamped his profile by doing one simple thing: trading out photos of himself for photos of a friend who was a former model. And who was in great shape. And who had never had any problems getting women. (Sting's words, not mine.)

We all see where this is heading, don't we? That's right: when Sting messaged the *same women* a second time, using the exact same profile with the exception of the photos, he got a response from *every single one of the women* who'd previously ignored him when he was using his own photos.

Did I panic a little when I read this? And worry that I might have been among those shallow women? Of course I did.

If you're familiar with the Old Testament, this was a lot like that prophet Nathan, tattling to King David that a rich man, with plenty of sheep, had stolen the one and only cute little sheep that was owned by the poor man. When David heard this report, he blew a gasket, raging that the man must be sentenced to death. He didn't realize that Nathan had in fact been describing *him*. Nathan knew that David was guilty of killing Uriah to steal his lone wife, Bathsheba. And in the wake of David's harsh pronouncement, Nathan announced, "You are the man!"

Pretty dramatic, huh?

I'm just saying that this guy's profile felt a little like that. And while I committed neither murder nor adultery, it was entirely possible that I might have ignored Sting until he posted "his" modeling pictures.

Ouch.

Please, Lord, don't let me be one of the women who ignored Sting. Was one of them me? Say it wasn't me.

Then my worries took on a life of their own.

Lord, please don't let Sting be writing a book about online dating. And don't let him mention "Margot" who's a "writer" in "Durham." Or google "Margot" who's a "writer" in "Durham." Because I'm super findable. Why did my mother name me Margot? Why not Amy? Why don't I live in a larger metropolitan area like New York City? Or Calcutta?

My anxieties can get pretty specific.

While no respectable part of me wants to *admit* that appearances are the most important thing I look for in a man, my "likes" and "messages" betray me. Some of my picks on Match.com aren't of men who have those iconic good looks found in Hollywood's leading gentlemen, but they're still not an unattractive bunch.

I confess this with wild reluctance because I'm very much aware that whatever wonderful man who will one day really dig who I am, and love God and people, and remain faithful to me, may come in a package that surprises me. In fact, chances are pretty high that whoever this unicorn is, he won't make the cover of *People* magazine's Sexiest Man Alive issue.

But whether or not I'm one of the women who ignored average- or below-average–looking Sting isn't really the point. The point is that this is how we operate. Unchecked, we judge people based on their appearances.

Sting's rant was really picking up steam and then he finally blasted his readers, saying, "So to all of you ladies who ignored me, but then responded to me when I changed my pictures, my advice to you is just to be honest and say that looks are what is most important to you and you can keep meeting up with the pretty men that have nothing else to offer. And please quit complaining that there are no good men out there because there are, but until you can get past a man's looks you will never get to know his heart and soul!"

It was very much a Nathan-the-prophet kind of moment.

We really are such animals, right? As much as we want to believe that we're people who make decisions based on sound emotional, psychological, theological, and moral reasoning, we are attracted to physically attractive people who probably *do* improve the human gene pool. *Curse you for being so right, Charles Darwin!*

And though being lectured is never my favorite thing, one of the talking points I think Sting got exactly right was that women should be *honest*. In fact, I think fessing up is the *only* way to get unstuck from this bind we've chosen for ourselves. I am honest when I confess that I am naturally drawn to physically attractive people. And once I've admitted it, I'm free to move forward and do something differently.

Noticing and confessing our natural impulses, desires, and temptations—and then asking God to help us see clearly—is the way to freedom. And it's why I'm a big fan of the all-purpose prayer that can so easily be appropriated for dating: *Lord, give me eyes to see.*

I hope you'll steal it.

As you're scrolling through profiles, pray, *Lord, give me eyes to see.*

As you're deciding how to respond to the guy who is into you and is a bit beyond your ideal age range: *Lord, give me eyes to see.*

As you're considering the faithful friend who'd like to date you but doesn't give you butterflies in your tummy: *Lord, give me eyes to see.*

It is a prayer that God loves to answer in all kinds of ways.

If he isn't Sexiest Man Alive attractive, maybe you notice that in one of his pictures he is wearing a Special Olympics volunteer T-shirt. (Man of my dreams, if you accidentally picked up this book in your sister's bathroom, now you know how to woo me.)

Or maybe he mentions serving as a Big Brother to a boy being raised by a single mama.

Perhaps he mentions his advocacy for that particular social issue that lights your fire.

Or maybe it's as simple as *seeing* and admiring the bend of his smile or the twinkle in his eye.

I am convinced that, in any number of creative ways, the one who opened the eyes of the man born blind delights in hearing and answering the genuine prayer of our hearts, *Lord, give me eyes to see.*

It's a prayer God loves to answer. And sometimes God is gracious enough to answer in easy-to-read font on our smartphones as we're reading a man's profile.

eight

KEEP YOUR EYES OPEN

Noticing the "Wins" in the Profiles You Read

Identifying what specifically draws you to a man's profile
helps you recognize the kind of man you're seeking.

When I started dating, I didn't know exactly what I was looking for in a man. Though, because my marriage ended after my
husband announced he was attracted to men, I had decided that
"heterosexual" would be a pretty high priority. It still is.

But maybe you're one of those gals who's created a list of what
you'd love to find in a mate.

You might have scrawled this secret list in a locked journal as a
teen or young adult, letting only your closest girlfriend steal a peek.
You may have prayerfully penned it in the back blank pages of your
Bible, or you may have been holding some sort of a list in your heart.

Though I don't have any hard data, I'm pretty sure this

age-old idea of a "list" began with the mantra "tall, dark, and handsome." That ancient gal had a really *short* list. But others of us have lists that are much longer. For some, Mr. Wonderful needs to be funny, have an IQ over 180, make a six-figure salary, and leap over tall buildings in a single bound. And in his free time he nurses premature bunnies to health.

You probably have noticed by now that creating a lengthy list of qualities you'd like to see in a man isn't instructed anywhere in the Bible. No, it's actually the stuff of rom-coms. But *even* in romantic comedies, the protagonist's plucky sidekick will eventually suggest that the heroine release her death grip on the list. Because it's obvious to everyone in the theater that the list isn't helping her find her Prince Charming.

Though I never created a list as a girl or young woman, my online dating experiences have unexpectedly led to creating something like one. When I began looking at men's profiles, I'd sometimes notice a golden nugget that really captured my imagination, or I'd notice something that I valued. Because I didn't want to forget them, I started jotting them down on a list I kept on my phone. These became my *noticings*. I wasn't intentionally looking for them in a profile or in a man I'd meet for a date, but when they appeared and I appreciated them, I'd pay attention and record them.

I'm not wed to this list, nor do I wield it as a list of nonnegotiables. It's simply a reminder of potential traits I'd like to find in a partner.

Here's a peek at some of mine.

"I HAD A GOOD MARRIAGE."

Many single women my age have a real appreciation for that widower who loved his wife, lost her, has been purposeful about grieving and healing, and is open to finding love again. We all seem to agree on this. (One of my friends actually met one of these unicorns on eHarmony and married him.) But another profile that stuck out to me was the guy who was divorced but noted that he'd had a good marriage. I don't know the backstory on that one, but because that is also my narrative, I have no reason to believe it wasn't true. I liked seeing someone who'd also experienced a good marriage. (Though no demerits for those who have not!)

"MY FAMILY IS IMPORTANT TO ME."

I appreciate when men either demonstrate or announce that their family is an important part of their lives. (Note: I do get a little miffed when a man proudly announces, "My kids mean the world to me." Honestly, unless you tell me that your children *don't* mean that much to you, I'm going to *assume* they do.) Sometimes the value of a man's family is evident in the photos he's shared and sometimes he mentions it explicitly. While I understand that some families are just difficult, I notice when a man values his family.

"I TAKE RESPONSIBILITY FOR MY SHORTCOMINGS."

While I don't think a brief profile is really the optimal place to fully explore and process the unraveling of a previous relationship, I do appreciate when—at some point—a man owns the failures in his past. I don't mean he confesses that a divorce was *all* his fault, but he also doesn't blame a broken relationship entirely on his ex—*both* of which would be red flags of caution for me. He does, though, take responsibility for his part, if not in his profile, then hopefully as you get to know him.

"I HAVE FRIENDS WHO ARE LIKE FAMILY."

Because many men my age haven't invested the time and energy to nurture relationships with other men, I'm always impressed and delighted by those who have. Maybe they've stayed tight with a group from college or maybe they are part of a small group of local men who meet weekly. In short, I value men who value their male friendships.

"I'M INVESTED IN A COMMUNITY."

At home in Durham, North Carolina, I have the holy privilege of living among folks with and without disabilities who've chosen to share life together. We're not under the umbrella of any agency; we are actually just a diverse neighborhood of many different adults and children who love each other and want to share life together. Of course, I understand that not everyone has the opportunity to be surrounded *geographically* by a loving community. However, I do value the choice, in whatever way it is lived out, to participate in a body where one is known and loved. Sometimes that happens in a church family. Maybe it's a men's group. Sometimes it's a very special neighborhood. Communities of love and support can be knit together in all kinds of ways.

"MY FAITH MATTERS TO ME."

While I'm not very picky about the way a man phrases it, I do want to know, beyond checking the "Christian" box, that his faith is an important part of his life. Whether he says, "God is my foundation" or "Jesus is the boss of me," I want to see that he prioritizes his faith in God.

"I KNOW WHO I AM."

While it gets a little dicey to quantify, I appreciate a man who's at least somewhat self-aware. Maybe he's a devotee of Brené Brown. Maybe he has six years of twelve-step sobriety. Maybe he's done some work in therapy. However it's lived and expressed, I like to see that a man is aware of how and why he is the way he is.

"I'M ABOUT SOMETHING BIGGER THAN MYSELF."

If SunBum919 is out on his boat every single weekend, he may not be the man for me. Do I hate a day at the beach? Au contraire, it's my favorite. But I'd much rather discover a man who invests in others by tutoring kids who are at risk than one who's consumed with the next weekend yacht party.

"I'M LIVING A LIFE I LOVE RIGHT NOW."

I am very dubious when a man who confesses to being a work-aholic says that he'll make time for someone special in his life. Maybe he will, but if he's not pausing to live a full life right now, what will be different when he's in a relationship? I love to read a profile of someone who already seems to be pretty satisfied with the life he's living.

"I'M FUNNY."

If a guy says that he's funny, or that he cracks himself up, or even that others think he's hysterical, I am reticent to believe him. But I love it when a man *shows* that he's got a good sense of humor by sharing a clever observation or snippet of self-deprecation in his profile. One kindred spirit announced, "Oh, and to the person or persons responsible for inventing peanut butter M&M's? I would like to kiss you full on the mouth. And then punch you in the throat." That funny bit caught my attention.

Those are my noticings of what I like to see in a man's profile, but of course yours will probably be different. (If you're the woman who's all about that boat weekend, I'll connect you with SunBum919.) But whatever is on your list, friend, I implore you to hold it loosely. Being responsive to what God is up to might mean giving someone you don't expect a chance. Stay open to the possibility that God could provide exactly the right man in unlikely packaging.

Since I've been doing this online dating journey, I've thought about the women I know who met their husbands online, and I realized that each of them was surprised by either a little something or a big something about the men who became theirs. Melanie hadn't dreamed of marrying a man who'd been divorced, but the husband she loves today was once married. Cora had never imagined she would meet a man who had mental health struggles, but once she fell in love she learned more about Dan's particular challenges and has gained skills to deal with it. Because Sharmaine's first husband had been a burly six-foot-five athlete, she had to adjust her expectations when God sent her an amazing man who had a more slight build. Beth hadn't imagined herself with an introvert, whom she describes as "thoughtful and deliberate," but today she is grateful for the balance her husband brings to their marriage. The right person might very well possess all kinds of qualities that wouldn't have made it onto your "list."

If you do have a list—maybe because you want to dazzle the guests at your wedding by proudly reading it to them at the reception—do me a favor, please. Whether you composed your list four months ago or four years ago, peek at it today with fresh eyes. Of the list of qualities you want in a man, ask, "What on this list does *God* prioritize?" I don't mean to overspiritualize this, and I'm not trying to shame you, especially not about prioritizing external qualities. (Unless, of course, your top priorities are that he has to be a billionaire ex-Chippendale model. In that case, maybe reexamine your focus, sister.) Rather, I want to help you notice who would be the best fit for you.

As I skimmed my list this morning through this lens, I felt confirmation in my heart that God and I *still* value someone who "knows and loves Jesus." The morning's peek also reminded me that while I'd love to find somebody local, for some very valid reasons, that's something I can hold loosely. When we ask, God helps us see.

I DID IT SO YOU DON'T HAVE TO

My Fat Fingers Accidentally Liked a Few Guys

Scrolling through profiles can be so tiring. So sometimes, late at night, I'd accidentally hit the smiley face, or heart, or "like," or thumbs-up icons when I didn't mean to. On one app, I could shake the phone vigorously back and forth and be given a do-over! Isn't that so fantastic? Unfortunately, on another app that didn't offer this magical feature, my rogue thumb accidentally liked Bruce's announcement that he enjoyed bacon, cheese, and the video game where people lose their lives called "Destiny 2" (well . . . two out of three!). Accidental likes happen. Move on.

COMMUNICATING WELL

The single biggest problem in communication is the illusion that it has taken place.

—*William H. Whyte*

nine

STARTING STRONG

The Two Things Every Strong First Message Must Do

A great message lets a man know that you see who
he is, and it gives him a chance to see who you are.

One evening you're rapid-swiping past profiles when one catches
your eye. Instead of the popular overly serious, sullen, pouty
selfie, this guy is smiling warmly in his cover photo. *Well done*,
Hopingifindyou. You quickly skim his profile, searching for any
obvious disqualifiers. If he lives in Australia, or is an enthusiastic worshiper of vampires, or is proudly polyamorous, your
work may be done for you. But a quick glance suggests this guy
actually checks some of the other boxes you value, which may
be similar to mine: local, Christian, and monogamous. So you
swipe through all of his photos. In addition to the obligatory

selfies, he's included a picture at the beach with his kids and the sweaty finish of a 5k run for a local charity.

Not bad.

So you carefully reread every word of his profile to make sure you didn't accidentally overlook a wife or a felony.

A spark of possibility flickers in your heart.

But now, the hard part: How should you engage?

This app gives you two choices: "smile" and "message."

The *win* of the smile is that it's safe. You don't have to risk much. The *risk* of the smile, of course, is that because it's a low-commitment signal, it's easy to ignore. Statistics prove that users are much more likely to respond to a message than to a signal like a smile or a wink.

Messaging takes more guts.

And the messages you've received from perfect, and imperfect, strangers have already taught you a few important rules about communicating online. When you message men, you don't want to go too small and you don't want to go too big. If you only sent one word—a standard "Hi," or the casual "Hey," or the stuffy "Greetings"—you've probably gone too small. You might as well have gone with the "smile," because you're not giving this guy anything of substance to which he can respond.

But if you send a lengthy diatribe that references your crippling lactose intolerance, or your cousin's ADHD diagnosis, or your ex's brand-new Ferrari, or what you don't like about your last therapist, you've gone too big. Then you're looking at a TMI (too much information) overshare.

Basically, it's the Goldilocks and the Three Bears situation again. Instead of going too small or too big, you want that first communication to be *just right*.

You not only want to use the right *number* of words, but you want those words to count. You want to make sure your message does two important things: it signals to someone else that you see who he is, and it gives him an opportunity to see who you are.

Does he love cycling? Suggest a local trail you enjoy.

Does he enjoy reading historical fiction? Mention a recent book you read.

Does he root for the Mets? If you're feeling sassy, make it clear you're a diehard Yankees fan.

It really is that easy. And you'll have done the two important things a first message should do: you'll have let him know that you notice him, and you'll have given him the opportunity to notice you.

And—this really is the icing on the cake—you will have made it super easy for him to respond. Super. Easy.

You glance at your watch, and it's 9:45. Late, but not too late to send a quick message.

You carefully type, "Hi Mike, I'm Jess. One of your photos looks like you're at Venice Beach in Southern California. I lived there in college and loved playing beach volleyball on Saturday mornings. It's nice meeting you."

Reread for typos.

Hit Send.

Way to go.

You did it.

And now you wait.

And try to sleep.

Messages that notice and appreciate who a man is and appropriately reveal who you are, are the kind of messages to which others want to respond.

Here are a few examples of messages I wanted to respond to, and why.

- "Good morning. I skate also . . . lol."
  One reason why: He noticed something in my profile that tells who I am, and he connected with it.
- "Good evening. It seems we have something in common. Zoosk and POF. Lol. I'm Joe. Hope all is well. BTW great smile!!!!"
  One reason why: He mentioned our common dating apps. He was playful. He was flattering.
- "Hey Margot, I'm a writer too."
  One reason why: He made a connection between who I am and who he is.

Do you see the common thread in the kinds of messages to which I wanted to respond? In each one a man noticed something about me: skating, smiling, writing. And I dug it.

The first person to draw my attention to this natural phenomenon, when I was about nine years old, was the blonde bombshell baroness in *The Sound of Music*: that sophisticated Elsa, who was competing with Fräulein Maria for the heart of Baron von Trapp. When Elsa noticed sparks flying between Maria and the baron, she called Maria out, "Come, my dear, we are women. Let's not pretend we don't know when a man notices us."[1] The baroness nailed it, right? Because when a man notices us, we *do* take notice. And if we're feeling him, we dig it.

There's something that is naturally compelling—in all kinds of relationships—about being seen, heard, and known. In a series of BBC radio talks broadcast during World War II, C. S. Lewis described what he called the "humble man." And while "humility" isn't quite as popular today as it was almost a century ago, Lewis described this type of person who's still very attractive today. It's the kind of person I hope you find, but more than that, I hope it's the person you'll aspire to be.

Lewis explained, "Do not imagine that if you meet a really humble man he will be what most people call 'humble' nowadays: he will not be a sort of greasy, smarmy person, who is always telling you that, of course, he is nobody."

I do enjoy his description of the stereotypical humble man being greasy and smarmy.

Lewis continued, "Probably all you will think about him is that he seemed a cheerful, intelligent chap who took a real interest in what you said to him."[2]

Did you hear it? He's describing a person who takes a genuine interest in others. No matter what century, no matter what gender, that holds up. When you're getting to know others, take a real interest in what they say in a profile, in a message, or over a cup of coffee.

Here are a few tips to keep in mind when you're crafting that first message in which you're aiming to do those two important things: signal that you notice who a man is and give him an opportunity to notice you.

- **Be Brief.** Some of the same reasons I gave when urging you to be brief in your profile description also apply to your first message. Too many words feel overwhelming to men. And to everyone. A sentence or two is plenty. You know the stereotype about women being effusive with our words and dudes being less chatty? Yeah, it's a stereotype for a reason.

- **Be Casual.** Don't tackle anything heavy. Keep your message light, friendly, and positive.
- **Be Observant.** If you connect with something a man has shared in his profile, let him know you're paying attention by commenting on it.
- **Be You.** Though it's tempting to want to labor over your words, and maybe even seem like someone you're not, to impress a man, just be yourself. It's better.
- **Be Discerning.** Don't share too much too quickly. It scares people.
- **Be Inquisitive.** A question, related to something you read in the profile, demonstrates that you're interested in who a man is. Be that person who takes a genuine interest in others.
- **Be Self-Assured.** Let a man know that you look forward to hearing back from him!
- **Be Conscientious.** Before you hit Send, proofread what you've written. It shows you care.

MESSAGING Q&A

Will I know if he's read my message?

Most sites have an indicator, like a little check mark, to let you know if someone has read your message. If you see that checkmark in your "sent mail," you know he's read it. (Because users can also pay an upgrade fee to be "invisible," there's also a chance he's read it and you'll never know. Ugh.)

What if he doesn't respond?

As a general rule of thumb, no response to your message signals that a man is not interested. And I hope you'll say to yourself,

That's okay. As someone who responds to only a small fraction of the messages I receive, I know there are a plethora of reasons I stay silent: they might have to do with what I read or saw on that guy's profile, or they might boil down to just what's happening in my life at the time. It's just the way the dating cookie crumbles. If a man doesn't respond to your message, you have two choices. You can let it go or you can message a second time. Some people find a follow-up message annoying, while others may admire your persistence. Any way you slice it, you don't have control over whether someone does or does not respond, so don't stress about it.

What if he does respond?

Sometimes polite men will respond to a message, answering a query bluntly, but they won't engage in a way that suggests they'd like to keep corresponding. If they don't follow up by taking an interest in you, let it go. More often, though, a response signals that a man is interested in getting to know you. If a response sounds and feels encouraging, take it as such.

As you're meeting someone new, have fun! Because if your relationship develops, trickier conversations are ahead.

HOW LONG SHOULD MY MESSAGE BE?

Aim to craft messages that approximate the length of his messages. If he's a one-sentence messager, aim for the same, at least at first. If he writes lengthier messages, feel free to answer in kind. Although strategic, this isn't "game playing." No, it's like a regular conversation over coffee where the best conversations have mutual give-and-take.

EMOJIS OR NO EMOJIS, THAT IS THE QUESTION

In a study of 90 million messages, the dating app Clover discovered that men are responding more often to first messages when an emoji is included.[3] But be warned: all emojis are not created equal. Men are replying to "okay" fingers, "crazy face," "laughing crying," "heart eyes," and "kissing lips." But they're less likely to reply to "engagement ring," "crying face," "Vulcan salute," and "pile of poo." So it's pretty much common sense. But avoid using too many emojis: research proves that those using too many emojis—and to be clear, anything in the double digits is way too many—are perceived as less intelligent.[4]

ten

LET'S TALK ABOUT
SEX, BABY

The Conversation You Can't Not Have

Know your own sexual boundaries and be
prepared to discuss sex with men you meet.

"What are your thoughts on sex?"

This was the text I received from a Christian gentleman I
was getting to know. And even though everyone loves to hate on
texting, the obvious beauty of the medium was quickly appar-
ent: I had time to think up an answer. Lots of possibilities raced
through my mind.

I think it's incredibly useful for procreation.

Looking forward to it, when the time is right.

I'm a big fan.

It's been awhile, but if memory serves, I'm pretty sure I remember how it goes.

Oh boy, I could entertain myself all day with these answers.

If I could have avoided having that difficult conversation, would I have? Probably. But avoiding it was no longer an option. And not just because an eager suitor had broached the topic. Discussing sex is requisite today for women and men who are meeting and dating—both those who claim Christian faith and those who do not.

Research shows that 33 percent of women have sex on the first encounter with someone they've met online.[1] So as you're getting to know a new man, even one who shares your faith, at some point you'll need to discuss sex. You'll want to know what his attitudes and expectations are, and he'll want to know what yours are. Whether you're gathering your courage to start the dating journey or whether you've been in it for five unsuccessful years, you need to be able to articulate your own personal convictions. And you will be best served and equipped if you pause to do that. Do it now. Right now. Don't pass Go or collect $200. I implore you.

Now is the best time, because a lot of the other times are ill-advised. Lingering together at your doorstep after a date isn't the time to figure it out. Sharing a glass of wine on his couch isn't the time for plan-making. (Sure, people do it, but those are some of the worst plans ever.) Now is the time. Write your plan where you can see it. Consider tattooing it on your forearm. If your forearm is already all inked up, I suggest putting it on your phone so when you're in the middle of the perfect date, you can sneak into the restroom at Ruby Tuesday to refresh your memory of the particulars of the plan. Do it now.

BEFORE YOU EVEN *THINK* ABOUT DATING, HAVE A PLAN ABOUT YOUR OWN SEXUAL BOUNDARIES.

I suspect you will establish different boundaries for yourself in relation to someone you're just meeting, someone you've dated regularly but don't yet know if a future commitment is forthcoming, someone you're dating seriously, and someone to whom you are married. (In fact, I'm counting on it.) Pray and seek God's wisdom on this, trusting that what you hear from God, which will always echo what you know from the Scriptures, is soaked in and dripping with God's big love for you. You decide when and how you will and will not share yourself, physically, with another.

BEFORE YOU BEGIN DATING, SHARE YOUR PLAN WITH A GIRLFRIEND.

Choose someone from your squad of gals who loves you, who can receive your plan, and who can support you as you execute it! Treat her to coffee and download the plan. This is the kind of information you don't want stored only on your own unreliable hard drive. If you spill a glass, or a bottle, of wine on that proverbial mental laptop—aka *your mind*—all data could be lost. That's why you really want it out there in the girlfriend cloud.

AS YOU BEGIN DATING, READ THE SIGNS.

If you feel awkward or uncomfortable talking about sex, you're not the only one. Men don't always know how to have a good conversation about it either. But that doesn't mean they're not thinking about, wanting it, or scheming how to get it. (Note to those who champion equality in all matters: this thinking/wanting/scheming group of humans doesn't *exclude* women. I hope you're happy.) Pay attention to cues a man offers. If he describes himself in his profile as "open-minded," or "passionate," or "romantic," he might be signaling more than bringing you flowers and chocolate. Also, it's kind of a joke in the dating world that when someone suggests an evening at home to "Netflix and chill," they're most likely not interested in having a cinematic journey. Read the signs.

TALK ABOUT SEX, WHEN THE TIME IS RIGHT, WITH THE MAN YOU'RE GETTING TO KNOW.

This is a conversation you can't not have. A girlfriend of mine, who is committed to waiting until she's married to have sex, has met over a dozen Christian men online and not one of them shared her value of waiting for marriage to have sex. So those conversations were pretty important for her to have. If you do *not* intend to have sex outside of marriage, then you need to share that. If you *do* intend to have sex outside of marriage, you also need to be able to articulate the kinds of expectations and boundaries that will keep you safe. Simply put, not discussing sex is an adolescent move that puts you at risk. A study out of the University of Texas reports that four out of five women don't use protection on that first online date. (Yikes.) In addition to using protection, one nurse practitioner offers a unique (maybe weird?) suggestion: creating a ceremonial date moment for partners to exchange results from recent STD testing.

A lot of online profiles, written by men and written by women, announce that the writer is looking for his or her "last first kiss." Whenever I read that, I breathe my silent agreement, "Same." A lot of us are looking for our forever person, and we're ready to get on with it. And while I won't ever write that corny thing on my profile, I may just write, "I'm looking for my last first conversation about sex."

A girl can dream.

NOTICING WHAT WE BRING TO DATING

All my life, men have told me I wasn't pretty enough—even the men I was dating. And I'd be like, "Well, why are you with me, then?" It's always been men putting me down just like my dad. To this day when someone says I'm cute, I can't see it. I don't see it no matter what anybody says.

—*Lil' Kim*

eleven

WHAT WE BRING TO DATING FROM OUR PAST

Moving Forward by Choosing What Is Most True

When we notice how our past impacts our
dating today, we can finally choose freely.

Each of us has a past, and it's influential in our relationships. Sometimes that past has affirmed our value and gifted us with healthy thinking patterns. Other times, though, it has infused us with lies that we need to reject.

THE LIE: *YOU'RE NOT WORTH SHOWING UP FOR.*

Here's the text I received, on a Friday afternoon, from Brett, the man I was supposed to meet for dinner that evening.

"Hi Margot, I hope you are having a great day so far. I had to make an emergency trip to Rocky Mount and won't make it back in time for our meeting. Will it be okay to reschedule for another date? I apologize for the late notice, but I just found out."

As far as canceling first dates go, Brett hit all the marks for being a pretty strong cancellation, nailing the most important ingredients:

- Extending a friendly greeting
- Taking a polite interest in me
- Referencing an "emergency"
- Suggesting that we reschedule
- Apologizing for the change

My friend Caroline also had an experience with a man who canceled their date.

He cited an "emergency" that kept him from honoring their plan to eat yummy food at Nana Taco. His excuse, though, was much more elaborate than the one I received—identifying the family member who had been hurt, detailing the nature of the injury, mentioning imminent plans to race to the emergency room, etc. His cancellation explanation was truly exquisite, and Caroline graciously released him.

Since Caroline was already hankering for tortillas, rice, and beans, she gathered a few of her girlfriends after work to join her for dinner at Nana Taco. As the gaggle of gals walked into the joint, Caroline glanced across the restaurant and saw the very fellow who'd canceled on her for the big emergency. He was out on a date with another woman.

With Caroline in mind, I couldn't help but question the

reason for Brett's cancellation. The fact is, I really don't know if Brett's cancellation was legit. Because it was vague, I don't know if his loving mother had a life-threatening stroke in Rocky Mount or if he was simply out enjoying delicious tacos with another woman. And as I was still weighing all the ways I could respond to Brett, the slightest wisp of a voice whispered in my ear, "You're not worth showing up for."

Wait, what?!

Who does that voice think she is, anyway, and why is she even involved in this situation? She doesn't know me.

Or does she?

Because what was happening inside me—feeling confused about why the longed-for other was not showing up, filling the void of not knowing by creating imaginary scenarios that allow my own sense of worth to remain intact—felt somewhat familiar. I've felt it before when I've thought about being born to a single woman who relinquished me for adoption. Though the longed-for other disappeared, I filled the void with imaginary scenarios of who she might have been. Or who my birth father might have been. Over the years, whenever I've had a thought that triggered that familiar feeling of rejection, I've quickly reasoned, "But they didn't even *know* me. They didn't know how awesome I would be to get to know in person." And while the logic worked, to convince me for a moment that I hadn't *really* been rejected, the feeling was *still there*, in my heart. The enemy capitalizes on our history, and the feelings it generates, to lie about who we are. And the naughty lie that accompanied my feeling hissed, "You're not worth showing up for."

We're all layered like that, and I heard that same sinister voice a few months ago when poor Brett had to cancel.

THE LIE: *YOU'RE NOT WORTH STICKING AROUND FOR.*

Then there was Frank.

Frank and I had been getting to know each other for about two weeks when we were finally able to nail down a time and place to meet in person. After I suggested The Pit, really talking up the local restaurant's barbecue and fried chicken and mac'n'cheese, I received this text, "Hey. My week has been crazy. I've been to The Pit. Love it. Met the guy that started the first one in Raleigh."

That he loved my choice of restaurants made me smile.

Two weeks earlier Frank had first messaged me, "Don't know if anyone made you smile today but wanted to say good morning in hopes it at least puts a little smirk on your face." Though I'm not a natural smirker, it made me smirk a little.

Frank broke the "photo attachment" ice by sending a pretty safe starter picture: "Here's my messy desk because I'm working so hard." Obviously, opening the door to photo attachments took the relationship to a new level. The next was a "Here's me at work" shot. He'd upped the intimacy even further by being *in* that photo. But the pièce de résistance? The golden goose of all photo attachments? A family picture taken at the beach of him and his three young adult sons. Sending a selfie is one thing, but sending pictures of one's *children*? That's the real deal. He trusted me to view his offspring.

I was really enjoying getting to know Frank when I received his "Work has been crazy, I love The Pit" text on Wednesday. Conversation had been a little light that week, but I saw no reason to worry since *work had been crazy*. We had plans. I had an outfit. What could go wrong?

Since we'd been chatting daily, I felt a wee bit uneasy when I didn't hear from Frank on Thursday. When I hadn't heard from him by late Friday afternoon, I knew I'd been ghosted.

Three girlfriends had been following the budding friendship, and I did text them to let them know the date seemed like a no-go. Emily called me to see how I was feeling. Olivia showed up at my window and invited me to sit in the rockers on her front porch, where she stayed present to my sadness, my hurt, my confusion. Around dinnertime, Lisa grabbed me for a big walk. Afterward I showered, and Olivia and I strolled downtown for a beer and greasy comfort fries.

By the time I got home that night—a very different night than the one I'd imagined—I'd logged eighteen and a half walking miles over the course of the day! But neither the endorphins nor all the French fries in the world could numb my sadness.

I tried to reason away the hurt, asking, "How could I feel so sad about losing someone I never met face-to-face?" And yet logic did not change the loss I felt.

Because something about it felt *familiar.*

When my adoptive parents divorced, when I was six, my dad left our home in Illinois to take a job in Connecticut. Though he was technically leaving my mom, my experience as a naturally egocentric six-year-old was that he was leaving *me.* But his departure was different from my birth parents leaving me behind. In their case, I'd always soothed myself with the thought, *They didn't know me.* They didn't know how awesome I was going to be.

My dad *knew* me.

But he still left.

The message that lodged in my deep places after my dad left was the naughty lie, "I'm not worth sticking around for." Because although my dad *did* know something about me, I reasoned that

I wasn't enough to make him stay. And Frank *did* know something about me—a lot, actually—but I wasn't enough to make him show *or* stay.

And just as I now believe intellectually that there was never anything I could have been or done as a child that would have made my dad stay, a small sane part of me knew that Frank's absence wasn't any reliable indicator of my worth. But in the midst of that sadness, I still heard that naughty lying voice that felt so familiar: "You're not worth sticking around for."

First Brett canceled. Then Frank ghosted. And in short order RonLovesGod rounded out the unholy trifecta of rejection.

THE LIE: *YOU'RE NOT WORTH KNOWING.*

Now, if Ron's screen name had been RonLovesCrack or GangstaRon or RonThePlayah, my natural healthy defenses would have kicked in to warn me, "Hey, girl, be a little cautious about this one." But the screen name RonLovesGod sort of lulled me into a bit of a discernment coma.

During the few weeks that we chatted, I did my due diligence and noticed a few red flags from RonLovesGod's past. But I was not going to be scared away by a few little flags. Maybe having somewhat of a shady past was the "big surprise" in God's good plan for me. But of course, I was also going to be discerning. The week before the date, I prayed, "God, if there's any legit reason for me to not eat a cheeseburger across the table from this guy, just let me know." I'd just gather more information over lunch to discern whether we'd be a good match. Because RonLovesGod lived about two and a half hours away, we decided to have lunch halfway.

Fifteen minutes after the time we'd agreed to meet, RonLovesGod had not shown up. He'd not called. He'd not texted.

God-loving Ron had stood me up.

Wait, what?! You are standing me up right now?

I didn't feel confused like I did when Brett had to cancel. And I didn't feel sad like I did when Frank ghosted. No, I felt indignant. And angry.

You are ditching me? After I was willing to roll with the red flags from your skanky past?

I'd felt that indignation before. When I was sixteen, my step-father of nine years left our home. He was an alcoholic. He was ugly to my mom. He was not an emotionally healthy individual. I was left by someone I didn't want to stay. And as I had been as an adolescent in relation to my stepdad, I was once again on the powerless side of the ridiculous equation.

And in RonLovesGod's absence, and Frank's, and Brett's, I heard the message with which I was all too familiar: "You're not worth showing up for. You're not worth sticking around for. You're not worth knowing."

THE LIE: *YOU'RE NOT WORTH LOVING.*

Though the sinister words had haunted me for years after my childhood, God had been so kind to heal my heart over the decade between my midtwenties and midthirties. In that gracious season God had convinced me I was beloved, and had whispered to my soul, "I am the One who is with you and for you." By the power of God's Spirit, I knew, in my deep places, that it was true.

I'd been enjoying that gracious healing work in my life for almost a decade when my husband left our home just before my forty-third birthday. Eighteen years into a pretty good marriage, I had been feeling solid and grounded emotionally. But that did not stop the deceiver, the one who lies, from poking at those healed wounds.

"What about now, Margot?" the voice hissed. "Are you worth loving *now*?"

Was I?

The sinister logic seemed to suggest, "If you'd been worth loving, he wouldn't have left." But he had. And in his absence, the voice that God had quieted began spouting off again.

You're not worth showing up for.

You're not worth sticking around for.

You're not worth knowing.

You're not worth loving.

And even though I knew better, because of all God had done in my life, the words still stung.

The brutal mantras had lodged in my deep places during a childhood that had included relinquishment, parents' alcoholism, and domestic violence, as well as the divorces between my adoptive parents and then between my parents and their subsequent spouses. And when my husband left, yet one more sinister mantra landed in my heart: *You are worthless garbage to be discarded.*

THE ENEMY OF OUR SOULS CAPITALIZES ON THE LOSSES IN OUR LIVES.

The way that the enemy capitalized on the early losses in my life is exactly how that uncreative little devil lies to me, and to you, about *dating*—insisting that we're not really worth loving. The deceiver capitalizes on the hurts of our past, twisting them to mar our present and destroy our hope for the future. Specifically, the voice that lies insists that we deserved whatever it was we got.

I don't presume to know exactly what this looks like for you. But I do recognize some of the ways it's expressed itself in my life and the lives of women I love when it comes to finding a partner with whom to share life.

- If we didn't date much—or at all—during or after high school, college, or grad school, the enemy hisses that there's something wrong with who we are that makes us undateable.
- Or if we dated a *lot* of men, the enemy accuses our hearts that we choose poorly or that we're not worth keeping around. Sometimes both.
- If we watched our friends get married and have children while we remained single, we are tempted to believe that we don't *deserve* the good they've received.
- If we harbor shame in our lives, about an abortion or sexual sin or abuse we endured, the enemy insists that we are unworthy of receiving good gifts.
- If we never knew our father, we might harbor silent suspicions that we're not worth knowing.
- If our appearance doesn't measure up to Mattel's Barbie doll, we mistakenly believe that we are insufficient.
- If we've been treated poorly by a man we've dated, we may not truly believe that we're worthy of protection and respect.
- If we are differently abled, or if we're different in a multitude of other less-obvious ways, we can swallow culture's lie that we're not enough.

I could go on. And so could you. The enemy's wily lies, rooted in our personal experiences, can keep us bound.

The reason I bring it up at all is to expose the crippling power of the voice that lies to rob us of hope and joy and possibility and confidence in God's goodness. But we don't have to stay stuck. When we expose the deceiver's dirty tricks, we can begin to see with new eyes. If we can agree that the enemy has come to steal, kill, and destroy—and that his weapon of choice is a lie—then we can identify that lie and replace it with truth.

WE CAN CHOOSE WHAT IS MOST TRUE.

I want to share what this looked like for me when my husband left. In that hollow void, the enemy took up residence in my heart, soul, and mind, chanting those naughty new words, "You are worthless garbage to be discarded." That was *the lie* I believed. I knew I had to hand that narrative over to God in search of what was *more true*. And when I did, God showed me a picture in my mind.

In this vision, I saw the big stinky green garbage buckets behind my house. And I noticed Jesus coming out of the back door of my home—which makes me think that's where he must live—and scooping me up out of one of those stinky buckets. I wasn't the big grown Margot I am today; I was a football-sized armful of baby-sized Margot, bearing all the hurts I was suffering. I actually do suspect that the loss triggered some of those earliest preverbal infant feelings about being discarded when I was relinquished. And in this mental picture, I saw Jesus cradling me in his arms. Delighting in me. Then Jesus spoke truth to my deep places, reminding me of what is most true about who I am: I'm worthy; I'm precious; I'm worth hanging on to. And from then on, I decided to choose what is most true. As I did, my suffering, under that crushing lie, subsided.

Was I carrying baggage from the past? I was. And even though I'd allowed God to deal with so many hurts from earlier in my life, I was being given another opportunity. Though it's not the efficient system I might have chosen for myself, that's just how it works sometimes. Kind of like the blind man Jesus healed in two parts. After the first touch, the man could see enough so that people looked like trees walking. And when Jesus touched him a second time, he could see clearly. And that's what God did when he replaced the lie about me being garbage with the truth that I was precious and worthy of love.

I hope I didn't make that sound like an easy formula for healing. There's nothing easy about facing squarely the pain of our past. But I do think that it's got traction. When we're willing to notice the critical events we endured, pay attention to the feelings those events elicited, and expose the enemy's lies, God is faithful to replace the lies we've believed with what is more true. And although the healing process requires work, I know one thing for sure: God's heart toward you and me is kind. When you gather up your courage and decide to discard the lies that are squeezing the life out of you, the Spirit is with you, guiding and supporting and blessing.

When we're scrolling through dating sites and considering possibilities, we can expect the enemy to interfere. But, graciously, we're not bound to be a victim of that interference. Although the enemy appropriates our history to lie about who we are, we have the tools to replace those lies with what is most true. The good news is that the One who made you also knows you and loves you. This is the voice to listen to. This is the face to trust. God is faithful to replace the lies of the deceiver with what is most true about who you are.

As you ask God to set you free, pay attention to the ways the deceiver attempts to capitalize off of what you have experienced to lie about who you are, who God is, and who others are. And as the Spirit opens your eyes to the enemy's lies, replace them with God's truth.

FINDING FREEDOM BY ROOTING OUT LIES AND PLANTING GOD'S TRUTH.

1. **Notice the Present Event**

   What was the event triggering your current feelings? Did you get stood up? Ghosted? Ignored?

2. **Name the Feeling Triggered by the Event**

   What was the feeling you felt in relation to the event? Anger? Sadness? Fear? Something else?

3. **Identify the Earlier Event**

   Was there an event from earlier in your life that resonates with what you experienced and are currently feeling? It might be a seismic loss, like the death of a parent. Or it might be a lesser event, like getting lost at a carnival, that is still stored on your mental hard drive. Ask God to open your eyes to what early event may resonate with the current one.

4. **Expose the Lie About You, Others, or God**

   What is the lie that the enemy is hissing to your heart?

This lie—about who you are, or who others are, or who God is—contradicts what you know to be true from Scripture. (You're not enough; he never loved you; God isn't interested in your suffering.)

5. **Claim the Truth About You, About Others, About God**

Finally, what is the truth—which will always resonate with what Scripture says about you, about God, and about others—that is more real than the lie that keeps you bound?

6. **Walk in Freedom**

Daily choose what God has shown you about what is most true about you, about God, and about others.

Beloved, I can vouch for God's faithfulness in this process because God has been so faithful to heal my own heart. One of the tools God offered me in that season was Henri Nouwen's book *The Inner Voice of Love*. During a particularly trying season in his journey, former priest and spiritual guide Henri Nouwen purposed to reject the lying voices and listen for God's true word, sharing those God-given affirmations in the book. He exhorts, "The root choice is to trust at all times that God will give you what you most need." And then he offers this beautiful, hard-won insight: "As you keep choosing God, your emotions will gradually give up their rebellion and be converted to the truth in you."[1]

They will. They really will.

And then you're free to let go of those old patterns that never worked before and try something new.

RECOGNIZE AND HONOR THE STRENGTHS YOU BRING FROM YOUR PAST

Each of us carries in our bodies the experiences that have shaped us. When we're dating, the wily lies from our past may sound a lot louder and bossier than the gentler good gifts we've also received. But those gifts are also worth noticing and naming. For example, during my first year out of college, my precious friend Geri gave birth to the most amazing little bundle of human life I'd ever encountered. His arrival taught me that I could love someone else's child fiercely, as if he were my own. So if I eventually develop a relationship with a man who has grown children, I know I have the capacity to love them well. Also, because I've faced losses, healed, and continued to flourish, I am carrying that resiliency into future relationships. Pause to notice the good gifts from your past that will help you thrive in a future relationship.

twelve

DOING IT DIFFERENTLY
THIS TIME

*Releasing the Old Patterns That Have
Never Worked for Us Before*

When we identify the old patterns of
relating to men that haven't worked for
us in the past, we can let them go.

At the beginning of my second semester of college, I was at a
basketball game when a young man I'd never seen before waltzed
into the gym. He may not have technically "waltzed," but I'm
pretty sure that I did hear winged celestial beings heralding
his arrival. And trumpets. As he climbed toward the top of the
bleachers on the opposite side of the gym, other students were
high-fiving him as if he were the prince of the land, returning

home from a voyage at sea. Or a semester in San Francisco. Whatever.

In an instant, I was smitten.

Who is he?

If you're not the rash, impulsive sort who makes snap love-at-first-sight judgments in the blink of an eye, I know that right now you're thinking I'm a few cards short of a full deck. I get that. And I respect it.

It wasn't the last time I'd get smote in an instant. It happened four-and-a-half years later at grad school orientation. My new friend Jill and I were walking to a dinnertime picnic welcoming all the new students to campus, when I noticed a tall, handsome man galloping across the quad with a small woman on his back. And in that magical moment, everything in me came alive. In an instant I knew that whoever the tall, dark, fun-loving guy was, I *wanted* him. So we got married and had three children together.

You're probably thinking, *Who's not playing with a full deck now?*

Me.

It's still me.

Can you see the pattern? At that time, the reasons for my love-at-first-sight pattern were unknown to me.

WHEN OLD PATTERNS ARE UNEXAMINED, WE REPEAT THEM

For the years we were married, my cute story about first laying eyes on my future husband, Peter, came off as quirky and charming when I tossed it out at cocktail parties. But when he left me after eighteen years of marriage to look for a man instead of a woman, I was forced to reckon with what wily, surreptitious force had drawn us together. Specifically, I had to ask what had drawn me in the twinkle of that magic moment. It took a while, and a bunch of therapy, but I finally figured it out: because I'd lived in a home with violence when I was young, I was drawn to men who were safe and definitely not violent. To my mind, this playful man with a woman on his back was clearly *not* a physical threat to women. I was attracted to that safe something in him at a completely subconscious level, hoping to get that need for safety met that my father had not been able to meet.

And what, you may be wondering, had happened in the moment when the boy-man who would become my college crush innocently stepped into the Murchison Gymnasium? Although I hadn't yet learned that he was a returning student who'd spent the first semester away from campus, I still recognized, in an instant, a man who "came back." Like I wanted my dad to come back from moving to a stupid job across the country. Or the way I wanted my birth father, whom I'd never set eyes on, to magically appear out of thin air.

Once again, lots of therapy.

A few months ago, my friend Olivia lent me the book *How to Get a Date Worth Keeping* by Henry Cloud. (You know that moment when you're writing a book on dating, and then your friend gives you a different book on dating, and you realize you are reading the very best book on dating that has ever been written in the history of the world? No? Me neither.) In it, Henry Cloud warns readers to notice and reject the old patterns that no longer serve us well. So when I notice my own patterns, I am all about Cloud's advice to do something differently. Because left to my own devices, I'll really screw things up. Truly, I sometimes think I should not be allowed to make any of my own decisions. But I'm convinced there is another way.

GOD HELPS TO IDENTIFY AND EXPOSE OUR OLD PATTERNS

We can identify and expose our old patterns so that we can finally conquer them. And this is where God's Spirit will help.

What the apostle Paul might call "lusts of the flesh," or "the natural man," I'd call "me left to my own devices." But the big promise of God is that, in the person of Jesus, we are no longer left to our own devices. In Jesus, God came to be with us and for us. And by his Spirit he opens our eyes to recognize the wily patterns that have kept us bound. The Spirit opens our ears to finally identify the voice that lies. Making us new is kind of like God's nine-to-five. And then five-to-nine. (In case you didn't get it, it's basically what God's up to 24-7.)

I don't know what particular set of fallen inclinations you've picked up on your journey. Clearly the self-preserving part of mine is the impulse to identify someone who is safe and reliable. And that's not all bad. There are worse impulses. The twisty part is when we're unaware of these impulses. Because while I did identify and even marry someone who was not a physical threat to women, I also chose someone who was attracted to men. That, of course, turned out to be a real bummer for both of us.

Maybe you're naturally attracted to that guy who's a bad boy.

Or you're a little bit turned on by the one who still smokes pot.

Maybe you keep choosing guys who don't treat you well.

Or perhaps you're tempted to keep going back to that one who hasn't respected you.

I get it. I really do.

And that's why I want you to hear that there is something, or someone, better for you than whatever it is your old patterns have driven you toward until now. This is your moment to make a different choice.

GOD HELPS US MAKE NEW CHOICES

Instead of saying, "I always go for the bad boy," try saying, "Up until now I've been attracted to this kind of guy. But now I'm making new choices." Can you hear the difference? Because your hurts and wounds are not who you are. God is healing you. God is equipping you. And God is guiding you.

Margot, are you really saying that when I'm scrolling through profiles, God's Spirit can guide me? Can open my ears to hear warning bells I've never noticed before and open my eyes to see green lights I wouldn't have otherwise noticed?

Yes, that's exactly what I'm saying.

That loving guidance could lead you to your Mr. Right. When that happens, I'll be your whole trumpet section. But more often, it looks much more mundane.

It looks like you finally having the idea and courage to send a little wink to someone who seems like he has a lot of integrity, but whose body shape isn't one to which you're naturally drawn. It looks like you being prompted to respond to a message from someone whose nationality isn't one you ever expected or imagined, because he seems to be a solid guy who took a real interest in who you are. Or it might look like you suddenly noticing something really remarkable about an Episcopalian if you're a Baptist, or a Pentecostal if you're old-school Catholic. Whatevs.

When God's Spirit began to open my eyes to the ways I was

attracted to men who were not the best match for me—because they were physically or emotionally distant, or because we were morally or spiritually mismatched—I was able to begin to make conscious choices to spend time with healthier individuals.

Ask God to guide you in releasing the old patterns that haven't yet worked. The kind of self-awareness the Holy Spirit grows in us can become a turning point that liberates us to make more life-giving decisions. And if you get stuck in this process, if you find it hard to broker change on your own, or with help from friends, ask your pastor to recommend a good local therapist. If you don't have insurance to cover the cost, providers can sometimes offer cut rates for those with financial need. However you pursue it—through journaling, or healing prayer, or therapy—God's good intention for you is to be free from the old patterns that have kept you stuck. And as we notice and expose the poor choices we've made in the past, we can discern the best way forward.

SEEKING DISCERNMENT

Trust in the LORD with all your heart and lean not on your own understanding; in all your ways submit to him, and he will make your paths straight.

—Proverbs 3:5–6

thirteen

READ THE SIGNS

Signals a Man Might Be a Good Match

You can recognize signs that a man
might be a good match.

Eventually I'd like to meet a man, develop a relationship, and get married. And by *eventually*, I mean *yesterday*. Have I swiped through profiles wondering whether this man or that one might possibly be "the one"? It's a little embarrassing to admit it, but yes, I have. It is what it is. Actually, it *was what it was* until a young woman I've never met helped me learn to ask a better question.

A church I've been attending has a prayer phone call every week for single women who are asking God to provide the right husband for them. (When I tell friends about it, I always start singing Beyoncé's "Single Ladies," but neither the church nor Queen B have authorized my unofficial appropriation.) The call includes a brief devotion, praying in the Spirit, and praying through specific prayer points together. A few months ago the call was led by a woman I've not met. She sounded young. And wise. At the beginning of the call, she shared a brief message about counterfeit bills that look real. As she spoke, my heart quickened. A counterfeit, she said, looks an awful lot like the original. But when you know what the real thing looks like, she shared, you can discern a fake.

As she spoke, I began to see, in my mind's eye, a number of the faces of men I've met on this dating journey. And I started seeing the ones who were, according to her rubric, not quite the real thing. None were posing. No one was pretending. But in each case, a part of me knew that they weren't quite "the real thing."

For me, the "real thing" is a man of God whom I can respect. He's demonstrated in his life the kinds of qualities that make for a solid long-term relationship. He has a track record of fidelity. There's evidence that he can go the distance. And while some of the men I'd met had lots of great qualities, I'd seen signs that some weren't the kind of solid, reliable man on whom I could depend.

When this wise young woman on the Single Ladies call assured us that God's Spirit gives us everything we need to discern the real thing from a counterfeit, it was as if she'd offered me a fresh new way of thinking about the men I'm meeting. She'd given me a tool for my tool belt. It's how I realized that "Is he the one?" wasn't the most helpful question at the *front end* of a dating relationship. I decided that a more useful question is, "Is he the real thing?" It's kind of like asking, "Is he the kind of person who possesses the qualities necessary to build something that will last?"

And when I asked that question, I began to notice other faces of men I'd met. These were the ones who'd given me reason to believe that they were genuine men of character. They weren't always the ones who dazzled me by launching successful nonprofits or being sports commentators for ESPN. But when I asked, "Is he the real thing?" again and again I recognized someone who was solid.

Although there's no sorcerous algorithm that can guarantee a good match, here are a few specific questions to ask if you're wondering whether a man is the real deal.

IS HE A PERSON OF CHARACTER?

Because I'm interested in meeting a man of character, I look for clues indicating that he might be: *Does he speak kindly? Is he caring for others? Does he value marriage? Is his faith integral to his daily life?* Ilene, a friend of mine, dated a man who told her that, to really discover who someone is, she should observe their character over a long period of time. Over time, Ilene did meet and get to know a man who demonstrated consistent good behavior and earned Ilene's trust. And, eventually, her hand in marriage. (It just wasn't the guy who gave her that good advice!) Look for a man who's a person of character.

IS HE EMOTIONALLY EQUIPPED TO NAVIGATE A MATURE RELATIONSHIP?

Not everyone walking around in a body that's thirty, forty, and fifty years old is an emotionally mature and psychologically healthy individual. That means that some men and women, who haven't done the work needed to grow emotionally, are not well-resourced to navigate the challenges of a long-term or short-term relationship. Notice whether a man is bringing tools—like skills needed for good communication, conflict resolution, and more—needed to build a healthy relationship.

IS HE INTERESTED IN DISCOVERING WHO I AM?

Notice whether a man is interested in discovering who you are. If you're on your first date and you aren't able to get a word in edgewise because he is talking about himself, it may not be the best fit. If you think he's just nervous, then give him some grace and go on that second date. But pay attention. As you're getting to know a man, notice whether he is interested in learning more about who you are.

DOES HE MAKE ROOM FOR ME TO BE WHO I AM?

You know how friendly dogs sniff each other's butts to see what's up? That's kind of what a first date is like. Metaphorically speaking, of course. Each of you is figuring out who the other is. You're sharing parts of who you are to determine if it's safe to fully be yourself. Pay attention to whether it feels okay to share your quirks. If you're tempted to minimize and hide who you are, though, proceed with caution. Or maybe don't proceed at all.

DOES HE VALUE WHO I AM?

When my ex-husband tells others who I am, both in my presence and out, he raves about my heart and my gifts. I mean, he is over-the-top effusive. (His new spouse can confirm this.) If I'm within earshot, I even start to believe that maybe I'm the most amazing creature to ever grace the planet. Although no one needs a partner who's blindly infatuated with her—to be clear, that's a really *bad* idea—it's fair to expect that the man for you will not only notice the unique woman you are, he'll *value* it.

COULD WE MAKE THE WORLD BETTER TOGETHER?

Tom, a neighbor of mine, was recently struck by a car when crossing the street. Within moments of the ambulance whisking him away, a couple in the neighborhood who loves Tom drove directly to the hospital to support Tom and his sister. That's because it's *who they are*. God had *good* in mind when he brought Don and Traci together thirty years ago. And though the "good" you will execute with a future partner might look different from the good to which Don and Traci are called, ponder how you and your potential match might be called to bless a world in need together.

In the absence of a magic love algorithm, keep your eyes open for these clues that might signal that a man is a good match for you. Look for a decent and emotionally mature individual—who knows, likes, and values who you are—who can walk beside you as you continue to become the woman God created you to be.

It's also not a bad idea to keep those peepers open for clues that you might be *attracted* to someone who's not the best match for you.

fourteen

ATTRACTION

What Charles Darwin Did and Did Not Know About Online Dating

Some of our attractions are conscious,
some are semiconscious, and others are
subconscious; we have the most freedom
when we can recognize all three.

In his national bestselling book *Blink*, Malcolm Gladwell explores a broad spectrum of choices that we make in a split second. Whether it's choosing a pint of ice cream in the frozen food section of the grocery store or connecting with someone online, the big idea is that the best decision-makers have the ability to "thin slice" the factors that matter most. It means they're able to make speedy inferences that are actually pretty accurate with minimal information. Gladwell observes that the enormous popularity of speed dating—an evening that often includes a series of six-minute conversations with about a dozen men—is proof of the effectiveness of snap judgment. Not to brag, but I could snap-judge no less than one hundred online profiles given those same six minutes. And yet for the hundreds of times I've snap-judged a hundred men, I'm still alone. And therein lies the problem. Gladwell confirms that my snap judgments simply cannot be trusted.[1]

And this is why I'm convinced that we benefit when we take the time to notice and name these different kinds of attractions. When we're conscious of what's driving our attractions, we are equipped to make good choices; when we're not conscious of what's driving our attractions, we are more likely to make poor choices.

WE'RE ATTRACTED—*CONSCIOUSLY*—TO THOSE WHO POSSESS ATTRIBUTES WE *VALUE*.

The top-tier kinds of attractions are those qualities we consciously prioritize as we consider potential partners. They're the ones on that list we talked about. They're the qualities we say we value: intelligence, fidelity, success, humor, faith. These are the attractive attributes we've consciously decided we value in a man.

WE'RE ATTRACTED—*SEMICONSCIOUSLY*—TO THOSE WHO POSSESS ATTRIBUTES WE *DESIRE*.

In addition to all the conscious reasons we might be attracted to a man, many of us also want to find what we call "chemistry." We're looking for someone who appeals to more than our minds and hearts. We want to feel that spark of desire for another person.

For a while I felt uncomfortable admitting I was looking for that spark, but eventually I decided to be honest with myself. While this may or may not be the kind of criteria I'll use to decide whether or not to be in a long-term relationship, it's an undeniable factor when considering a man's initial appeal.

There's no shame in noticing that this is how we're wired. We're naturally attracted to those who are naturally attractive. I feel fairly certain the nineteenth-century naturalist Charles Darwin wasn't thinking about online dating when he said that each species advances when the characteristics that make it most likely to survive and reproduce are naturally selected. For instance, think about early cavemen, specifically those with quick legs and strong spear-throwing arms. You know the cave babes dug those dudes, because they could bring home the bacon. Oh, and . . . natural selection. I'm not saying we're *animals*, but many of us do demonstrate a preference for the kinds of qualities that would naturally come in handy with essential tasks like survival—and reproduction. Some of us twenty-first–century gals who are beyond our prime childbearing years are still attracted to these graying hunks and just haven't gotten the memo that a slow man who can't throw a spear will most likely work out just fine.

Today these primal attractions could include a desire for financial security, which might find expression in being drawn to a man wearing a class ring from Yale, pocketing a thick wallet, or sporting a tailored Armani suit. One study found that men who reported incomes higher than $250,000 in their online profiles received 156 percent more messages than those who reported incomes of $50,000.[2] Just sayin'.

So as we scroll through hundreds of online profiles, some of us make decisions that are based on attributes we *desire,* of which, I believe, we're only semiconscious.

WE'RE ATTRACTED—*OFTEN SUBCONSCIOUSLY*—TO THOSE WHO POSSESS ATTRIBUTES WE *KNOW.*

Many women are attracted to qualities in men that we've *experienced* in our previous relationships, particularly in our families of origin. The pattern called the "familiarity principle"[3] is accepted and well-documented in the field.

My own formative experiences were with a birth father who was an imaginary ghost, an adoptive father who was dangerous until he got sober, and a stepfather who was, until he left, drunk more often than not. It's why I now think that the guy who's way out of geographic reach is intriguing. Or the man who texts me every morning to say good morning but can't make time to meet in person has all the right stuff. And the guy who had at least four liquor drinks during our lunch date? Magnetic. And the man who was grieving, still loved his wife, and was not yet ready for a relationship? Are you kidding me? He was absolutely irresistible.

Gentlemen readers, if you are geographically, physically, mentally, spiritually, philosophically, or emotionally unavailable, you can bank on the fact that I will find you wildly attractive.

This temptation to gravitate toward what we've known isn't reserved for those of us with fathers who are obviously dysfunctional or undeniably absent. A girlfriend of mine, who I'll call Dee, had a very respectable Christian father and she noticed this same tendency in herself. Because, *therapy.* Dee's dad always remained married and faithful to her mom, was physically present in their home, and never once verbally or physically assaulted anyone. But he was also a man who was very driven to pursue success and power. Since I'm not his therapist, I won't diagnose him, but it's evident to those who know him best that he possesses qualities that many narcissists possess. And it wasn't until Dee's marriage was unraveling that she was able to recognize that she'd "ended up" with a man who turned out to be wired very much like her father.

Thankfully, in my rigorous research to get you the very best intel on why we make the dating choices we do, I was given the opportunity to interview one of today's bright minds who really helped me understand why the power of our attractions actually goes beyond *familiarity*.

Q&A: WHY AM I ATTRACTED TO MEN WHO AREN'T THE BEST FOR ME?

On the way to an out-of-town trip for a writer's conference, I requested an Uber to pick me up at 5:30 a.m. to take me to the airport. As I sat on my front steps beside my rolling suitcase, I continued to noodle on this "familiarity principle," wrestling to understand why I'm attracted to guys who are too far away, or too unreliable, or too disinterested. Within moments of hopping in the back seat of Len's lime-green Prius, I discovered that he was a doctoral candidate in relational psychology.[4] So it sort of felt like *God* had sent him. As we chatted, nothing Len said made me doubt it.

> **Margot:** Len, have you ever noticed that some women are naturally attracted to guys who are not the best guys for them?

Len: Yes. We are attracted to people who remind us of the parent who gave us the hardest time growing up. We are especially attracted to that parent's negative traits because that's what caused the most emotional damage. Then, when a potential suitor presents those characteristics, we are unconsciously attracted to that person in order to try and get it right this time around— and to get the emotional nutrition we justly deserve.

Margot: Whoa. That's remarkable insight. It really explains so much—that we're still trying to get those unmet needs met. I think I can probably guess your answer, but does that ever really work out?

Len: Not very well. Since opposites do attract—narcissists and codependents, those who were smothered and those who were abandoned, introverts and extroverts—our old brains are trying desperately to reconcile the pain from the past. But the results don't meet our expectations and then we want out of the relationship. One of the reasons these particular breakups are so devastating is that our old brains believe that if we separate from our abusive partner, we will die. Many couples stay in these abusive relationships clinging to the hope that the surrogate mom or dad we're in the relationship with will eventually come around and be nice to us.

Margot: This is crazy, Len! Why on earth do I—I mean why do *other* poor suckers—do this?

Len: So we can play the familiar role from younger years! Again, we are attracted to parental figures. How many times have you heard someone say, "I feel as though I've known you all my life"?

Margot: And what are the signs that we—I mean "they," obviously I mean "they"—might be doing that? How do we recognize it?

Len: It's difficult to do because the attraction is unconscious and fluid.

Margot: Uh-oh. How or when do we snap out of it?

Len: As soon as those love hormones wear off: dopamine, oxytocin, vasopressin, epinephrine, serotonin. When those hormones are flowing, you don't defend yourself. You let slide things that would ordinarily get on your nerves. You don't think critically. But when you find yourself questioning the merits of the relationship, that's the time to see a qualified professional. Get an outside opinion. Get out of your own head!

Margot: So is there any hope to do it differently?

Len: The right person for you might be someone you consider boring. Because if you cannot play a familiar role, you will perceive him as boring.

Margot: I really do not see myself choosing someone like that. But say some more. Try to convince me, Len.

Len: "Boring" is kind of like magnets with similar polarities: they *repel* each other. When someone says, "Well, he's nice, but . . ." it means there is no parental prototype with this person so I can regain all that I lost in childhood. Therefore, a relationship with this person will not help me to resolve the issue I had with the parent who gave me the hardest time.

Margot: Oh boy, Len, you've given me a lot to chew on. You have truly been my angel driver sent by God. Thank you.

Reader girl, it's pretty obvious why I suspect divine intervention, right? Len's insights have changed the game for me. Forever.

Bottom line: There's a lot about ourselves that we don't see . . . until we see. And there is fabulous potential for growth and transformation on this dating journey when we're willing to review some of the bad choices we've made in order to break the old patterns that have kept us stuck. We can begin to do that by asking God to show us the ways we've been attracted to what's familiar. This isn't about blame or faultfinding. It's about recognizing the ways in which we may still be attracted to what we experienced that might not be optimal for us. That's the big win.

And when we know what's going on inside ourselves, we're better equipped to decide if, in this particular season, dating has our name on it.

fifteen

FIRST THINGS FIRST

The Secret That Fierce Single
Mama Bears Can Teach Us All

If dating is what God has for us in this
season, God will meet our needs.

Dating while my offspring were in their late teens, my biggest
concern as a single mom was that I might cross paths with one
of them at the mall. *Nobody* wanted that, so we all found ways
to avoid it. But moms who are parenting younger children who
not only need them in all the ways but who still actually *enjoy*
spending time with their mommies can face some unique challenges while dating.

When I talked to Single Mama Bears who were dating
while parenting young cubs, their concerns about dating—not
surprisingly—all hinged on being able to continue parenting

their little ones well. They wanted to ensure that their cubs were receiving protection, nurture, provision, and presence. And what Mama Bears know intuitively about caring for their cubs is the kind of self-care every one of us—who may or may not yet be convinced we *deserve* it—can offer *ourselves*.

The most primal worry I heard from Single Mama Bears who dated while their kids were young was a fear of welcoming someone potentially dangerous into their children's lives. Of course, moms were very slow and deliberate about introducing someone new to their children. Because our job is to protect our cubs, we make sure that dating doesn't interfere with that.

The second weightiest concern I heard from dating moms was for the *nurture* their children were receiving. Moms worried,

- "I fear my dating will negatively impact my kids who already don't have a consistent father figure."
- "I fear I'm taking valuable time away from raising my kids, so that I'm not spending quality time teaching them *everything* they need to know."
- "I fear that because I don't have a spouse, I'm not the best I can be for my kids."

We do the best we can do, right? We either hold off on dating for a minute, or we find solutions to ensure that our kids' emotional needs are met. Though it requires creativity, it's possible. Because our job is to nurture our cubs, we make sure that dating doesn't interfere with that.

Third, Mama Bears noted that, even if you never have to pay for a single piece of pizza or bucket of popcorn, dating can be expensive. For moms who don't have family nearby to help care for their children, the cost of babysitters adds up quickly. Like *in one date* quickly. And because we're moms, when it comes to dollars and cents, we naturally prioritize our children's needs over our own. But there are creative solutions. Like enlisting that fierce support squad of gal pals who love our babies and are itchy to give baths and read bedtime stories. Because our job is to provide for our cubs, we make sure that dating doesn't interfere with that.

And, finally, every Mama Bear named *time* as the limited commodity that made dating as a single parent the most challenging.

- *Getting* a date takes time: One mom acknowledged the toll it takes. "As the sole parent I don't want to spend my evenings texting and dating," she said. "Once a week, yes, but heavens, I'm really busy with this life; adding a second one is exhausting."
- Going on a date can be *trickier for moms* than for dads: If your children's father has died or is uninvolved, everything is trickier, right? And in many divorces, fathers' schedules are disrupted a bit *less* than mothers' schedules. (*Broad sweeping generalizations anyone?* Yes. And facts.)
- *Going* on a date takes time: One mom noticed, "It's crazy trying to align the stars for four hours of adult time."
- Going on a date is sometimes simply *impossible*: At some point, a cancellation will be necessary. When one mom canceled her afternoon date, she was calling him from an urgent care center where her previously bleeding daughter was getting twenty-two stitches to sew up a gash in her leg. The gentleman who'd been looking forward to their plans

was a little miffed. "She's stitched up now," he demanded. "Why can't you make it?" Clearly, he's not a mom.

If you're completely bummed out now, remember that if dating is what God has for you in this season, God will provide. With amazing grandparents. And friends who adore your children. And families at church who love you and your kids.

One mom named the lunch date as the big win for Single Mama Bears. If your kids are in daycare or school, a lunch date could be the big win. As one mom confided, "No one needs to know. Your neighbors don't need to know. Your colleagues don't need to know. Your parents don't need to know." If it goes really well? Awesome. If it goes really poorly? Eat your burger and go back to the office. You didn't have to hire a babysitter. Because our job is to be present to our cubs, we make sure that dating doesn't interfere with that.

Whether we're women parenting little ones or not, a lot of us are asking whether online dating has our name on it in this season. And I think the concerns of these moms of young ones point us to the answer: when our basic needs are met, as well as the needs of those who depend on us, we're in the best possible space to be dating. Make sense? It's like *we* are the cubs who deserve to have our needs met. The care that we're convinced our children, or nieces and nephews, or other little ones *deserve* is the same care we must offer ourselves. Each of us will have the best experience of dating when our physical, emotional, and spiritual needs are met.

And when we do decide the moment is right for dating, we'll gather up our courage for the journey ahead.

sixteen

COURAGE

Taking a Risk and Trusting God

A valuable tool for the journey is
choosing to take Spirit-led risks.

About a year ago I was roller-skating at American Tobacco Trail when I noticed a guy, around my age, who was out for his Saturday morning run. One week we smiled at one another. The next week I waved. The next week he cheered for whatever team I had emblazoned on my T-shirt. I think the young people call this "flirting." After a few weeks of this, I made up my mind to introduce myself. When I saw him approaching, I gathered my courage and slowed my roll to say hi.

"Hi," I said, trying to act normal. "I'm Margot."

Nailed it.

Pausing from his run, extending his hand at the end of a very muscled arm, he smiled and offered, "Hi, I'm Matt."

"Well, it's nice to meet you!" I chimed, spinning around to keep skating. "Enjoy this beautiful day."

And that was that.

Except that after that, when our paths would cross, we'd pause to chat. Sometimes I'd turn and skate in his direction for a bit while we talked. Although Matt was ultimately not the guy for me, I feel really proud that I took a risk. And that baby step taught me that I could be brave.

I realize that not everyone is cheering for my big braveness. Those who believe a woman should wait around quietly to be "found" by a man who's searching for his good thing could easily dismiss my brazen introduction as failing to trust God. But I see the exact opposite: everything about meeting Matt required me to trust God.

EXERCISING COURAGE TO TAKE A RISK IS ONE WAY WE ACTIVELY TRUST GOD.

Dating necessarily involves taking a risk. Ten percent of online daters quit after ninety days.[1] And 33 percent of people who've used online dating sites haven't ever met up with someone they met there.[2] Maybe that's you. While there are endless possibilities to explain why that is the case, one of those many reasons could be fear. It takes courage to put ourselves out there!

Throughout the Bible, God invited men and women to do something that was a little bigger or a lot bigger than what they could do without God's help. Moses, Noah, Hannah, Mary, Elizabeth, Jesus, and others all took a risk by doing something big when they depended on what God provided. Not for a moment do I think that flirting with a handsome someone is on par with—oh, let's say—rescuing humanity by either building an enormous boat or bravely bearing the Savior of the world. That would be crazy. But I do think that because God can be trusted with every single area of our lives—dieting and doctors and dollars and dating—God can certainly be relied on when we take a calculated social risk.

STEPPING AWAY FROM A RISK IS ANOTHER WAY TO ACTIVELY TRUST GOD.

To be clear, trusting God doesn't mean that we are always mechanically called to *do* the big thing that we wouldn't be able to do on our own. We don't mindlessly take a risk just because it presents itself. Sometimes we trust God by stepping away from the risk. That's what Jesus chose in the wilderness, when Satan taunted him to use God's help to turn a stone to bread. Rather than take matters into his own hands—at a moment when, I can't help but notice, he was super-duper hungry for the good thing—Jesus exercised trust in God by *not* attempting the thing that required God's helping power. So, on a different day when I'm roller-skating, I will put my trust in God by *not* going out of my way to meet a guy.

Are you tracking? Sometimes we trust God by taking a risk; sometimes we trust God by stepping away from a risk. And while I can kind of hear how it sounds like a fancy way of saying absolutely *nothing*, if we really believe that God is actively guiding us, then responding to God's moment-by-moment leading to step out or stay put is the bravest thing we can do.

Let's say that there's a man at church in whom you've begun to have an interest. You've chatted a bit and seem to be interested in one another, but your friendship has thus far been limited to a few conversations within a fifty-yard radius of the sanctuary. As you trust God to lead you, God might ask you to pause and not initiate plans at that time. You might not even know why, and that's okay. Or, the Spirit might prompt you to step out and invite this man to grab some lunch after the service. Sometimes we trust God by *not* risking, and sometimes we trust God by risking.

AS WE OBEY GOD, WE GROW IN OUR ABILITY TO DISCERN AND NAVIGATE POTENTIAL RISKS.

My therapist friend Meredith, who met her husband on eHarmony, is one of the strongest, bravest women I know, and she describes dating as that arena where she was able to grow as a person. She reports, "I got more comfortable taking risks and putting myself out there. I learned how to tell a guy to his face that I didn't want to go out again. I learned how to be clear and not just nice." Her willingness to be transformed by God challenges me to take risks that will help me grow.

Wherever God's Spirit is guiding you, I'm inviting you to take one little baby step. It might be a step forward and it might be a step back. Both take courage! And even if nothing comes of your brave obedience, as was the case for me, obedience still goes in the book as a win.

Assured of God's steadfast presence and leading, you can even weather some of the trickier twists and turns on the journey.

DISCERNMENT EXERCISE

As you consider a particular situation you're facing in dating, ask God to guide you. One helpful question is, "God, is it more faithful for me to move forward, to stay put, or to step back?" Then trust that God's Spirit can, and does, illuminate your heart and mind.

PRACTICING SELF-CARE WHILE DATING

Secure your own mask first before helping others.

—*International Civil Aviation Organization*

seventeen

RED FLAGS

*Warning Signs You Can't Overlook and
What You Can Learn from Them*

When you notice red flags in a
man's profile, exercise caution.

Sometimes I've found myself reading a profile and beginning to feel uneasy. Other women have told me about going to that first meetup and sensing that something was a bit off. Their gut was churning, but they couldn't put their finger on exactly why.

For starters, you don't need a reason; give yourself permission to just trust those instincts. But if it's helpful for you to name *why* a particular person might be turning you off, here are a few potential red flags.

A MAN IS OVERLY EAGER TO MEET.

After exchanging just a few messages in rapid succession around nine on a Saturday night, a new friend, who lived about fifteen miles away, asked, "Are you in for the night?" While he may have had the very best of intentions—and really, who can blame him for being immediately smitten by yours truly?—our rather mundane messages just weren't reason enough to warrant an *immediate* face-to-face meetup. The speedy pace made me wonder if he was after something other than a great conversation. (After declining the late-night rendezvous, I never heard from him again. So I feel good about my decision.)

Response: While there's no hard and fast rule about when to meet in person, notice what your gut is telling you and respond accordingly. If you're not comfortable meeting face-to-face so quickly, then don't. Wait until you're ready.

A MAN IS OVERLY RELUCTANT TO MEET.

Things were really clicking along with one man I met online. We had a good vibe and enjoyed communicating. One month of texting led to the next. And then the next. And then the next. Because I really liked him, I put up with this . . . pace . . . for longer than I should have. It took three months, after what felt like a lot of nagging and begging on my end, to finally meet face-to-face. After that meeting, though, we fell into the same reluctant pattern again, communicating regularly but not spending time together. Eventually I chose to end the friendship, since I was looking for more than a pen pal.

Response: Actions speak louder than words. If a man isn't ready or willing to meet face-to-face, it may be time to move on.

A MAN IS TOO NEGATIVE OR DEMANDING.

Some fellows have very clear ideas about who they're looking for and who they are decidedly *not* looking for. You'll know this when they say things similar to this:

"If you don't look exactly like your pictures, don't contact me."

"If you are a religious fanatic, stay the hell away from me."

"I want a woman who can maintain a house with high, clean standards of living."

Well, kind sir, I'm out. Definitely on the third, but possibly guilty of the first two as well.

Response: Exercise caution before entering into a relationship with a man who's overly negative or demanding.

A MAN IS TOO IDEALISTIC.

When asked what he was doing with his life, one gentleman wrote, "Work, work, work!" He went on to say that he was hoping to find someone with whom he could play, play, play. And maybe he will. But if his life is that focused on his work now, isn't it a bit idealistic for him (and me) to believe he'll be different when he's in a relationship?

Another gentleman offered, "I want to find someone who can complete me." That may have been poetic language used in a popular movie, but it also gently suggests that he currently views himself as being incomplete and possibly is a bit too needy.

Notice the subtle cues by which a person suggests that he will be different, or somehow *better*, in a relationship than he is now.

The reality is, he probably won't.

Response: As you consider getting to know someone new,

assume that he will continue to be the person he already is. He will not become suddenly different when he's in a relationship, and you certainly will not change him so that he, immediately and permanently, behaves differently than he already does.

A MAN HAS AN UNREALISTIC VIEW OF RELATIONSHIPS.

One man honestly admitted, "I like to spend time with my lady as long as she is happy." As a lady, I also find happiness appealing, but since no one is always happy, including me, the natural converse of his announcement is troubling: If she's unhappy, then I'll drop her like a hot potato. No thank you.

Response: Choose a man who understands that expressing feelings need not threaten a relationship. In fact, healthy relationships make room for partners to experience a variety of feelings in a safe space.

A MAN SHARES PHOTOS THAT CONCERN YOU.

On one site, I came across a profile that troubled me. A gentleman had uploaded four photos to his profile. The first two were close-ups of his face. The third looked like a stock photo of a woman whose hands were bound together over her head with rope. Call me paranoid, but that seemed like a red flag. The fourth photo showed seven or eight skeins of rope, leaving me to wonder what they might be used for. I don't think it was rock climbing.

Pay attention to the pictures. If he's holding a joint in every picture, or has different scantily clad women hanging on him in each shot, I believe you can safely deduce something about him. Not everything, but *something*.

Response: Because a picture is worth a thousand words, men who share disturbing photos have given you a lot of valuable information! Heed it.

A MAN REQUESTS PHOTOS THAT CONCERN YOU.

If a man requests revealing or otherwise inappropriate photos from you, or sends his own, it's like he's done your job for you. He separated the wheat from the chaff. For that, chaff, we thank you.

But some requests may seem to fall into a gray area.

One afternoon I was chatting with a guy who seemed really interesting. In fact, we'd made plans to get together the following afternoon to shoot hoops in a public park. How fun is that?! The following morning, he asked for a morning selfie. (This gentleman was a little bit younger, and I don't think he had a very good grasp of what a forty-nine-year-old woman can look like first thing in the morning.) I was still noodling on the uncomfortable request when he messaged again, asking for pictures of . . . my toes.

And then I was done.

Response: As a relationship unfolds, it may be perfectly fine to share a few extra pictures. Even pictures of all your digits. But if he requests specific types of photos (only fifteen hours after your first message, in my case), then you might want to put a hold on the relationship—possibly forever.

A MAN AND YOU HAVE DIFFERENT OBJECTIVES.

One site I tried asked users to name what it was they were after: short-term dating, long-term dating, marriage, and so on. I'd hurried through creating my own profile, so I hadn't read all of the options. Then I came across CowboyBob67's profile, and it left me scratching my head.

Part of his profile said, "CowboyBob67 isn't seeking a relationship or any kind of commitment."

If we'd been on a site called "Single People Who Want to Stay Single," his choice would have made more sense. But since we were on a dating site, I deduced that "isn't seeking a relationship" was actually code for "is only seeking a sexual relationship."

CowboyBob67 was not the cowboy for me.

Response: Like the men who post or request troubling photos, those who say they're looking for a one-night hookup, or an extramarital affair, or an extra person to join their marital union have made your job of discernment pretty easy. Thanks, guys!

A MAN HAS A SCREEN NAME THAT CONCERNS YOU.

I mentioned that screen names—whether bland or descriptive or nasty or playful—can reveal something about a man. Some names dampen my interest immediately, including these:

- ComfortablyNumb
- Idkwhatimdoing
- TROUBLE
- Twisted
- Nasstyl

As my friend Hitch, the date doctor—aka Will Smith in the movie *Hitch*—says, "You only have one chance to make a good first impression."[1]

Response: Consider swiping left. However, keep an open mind. Just in case ComfortablyNumb is an anesthesiologist.

A MAN REVEALS INAPPROPRIATE VULNERABILITY.

One fellow, who no doubt meant to be clever, chose to lead by highlighting his bumpy past in his headline, declaring, "Two decades of getting it wrong."

To me, it precariously straddled the border between "really clever" and "a little concerning."

Another began his profile, "Why doesn't anyone like me?" That one landed squarely on the side of "concerning."

A third caused me to close the app completely:

"Notice to readers: The member has died, of loneliness. Autopsy found his heart has shrunken due to lack of love and has several breaks around the exterior. Further inspection found frostbite of the eyes, ears, and hands with a direct correlation to online dating sites, atrophy of the lips due to decades of unuse."

I value vulnerability as much as the next gal—but only if it's in an appropriate *context*. The one-thousand-characters-to-introduce-myself at the start of a profile is decidedly *not* the right context.

Response: If a man reveals inappropriate vulnerability, notice what your gut is telling you. This isn't to say there's no room for vulnerability in profiles. A great example, in my mind, is someone who's in recovery from some kind of addiction. For a variety of reasons—that include, but are not limited to, *my cool dad*—I think people in recovery are some of the best humans on the planet. So I have mad respect for a self-aware man who shares on his profile that he once battled addiction but that he's been clean and sober for twelve years. To my ear, that demonstrates self-awareness and fortitude. And it feels like an appropriate expression of vulnerability.

A MAN'S PROFILE HAS POOR GRAMMAR AND MANY MISSPELLINGS.

As a literary professional, I confess that I feel like a word snob for even *mentioning* this. But because it's *also* one of the profile-improving tips offered on a popular dating site, I've chosen to reiterate it here.

Profiles with many misspellings and grammatical errors reveal something about a person. When someone who struggles with grammar and spelling crafts a job résumé, they have a nerdy friend, like me, read it over. They polish a résumé because it is a reflection of them, and *it matters*.

Other than the photos a dude uploads—the gym selfie in front of Planet Fitness's signature purple and yellow walls, or wearing camo and posing in a tree stand with his favorite automatic weapon—a man's written profile is the *only* information you have to help you decide whether you want to learn more or head for the hills. (And no one forced the camo-wearing guy at gunpoint to write it in less than thirty seconds. If he'd wanted to make a solid impression, he could have asked for help.)

Okay, end of snobby rant.

Beyond suggesting that he just didn't try very hard, some errors also leave the writer's meaning open for interpretation.

HighFlyin1970 wrote that he was looking for a "sweat loving woman." So the recipient of this message, my friend Van, was forced to wonder, "Was his affinity for his own perspiration, or was he looking for a mate with active sweat glands?" #spellingmatters

Another fellow said he was looking for "a professional dependent person." I want to believe he meant *independent*, but maybe there was something in him that desperately needed to be needed. We'll never know.

Response: Because writing is not every person's forte, you may choose to practice generosity by overlooking errors. If so, you will still want to remain alert for the other red flags described in this chapter.

A MAN ISN'T ABLE TO BE HONEST ABOUT HIS PAST.

When I asked one man why his marriage ended, he offered the very easy answer, "We grew apart." *Maybe.* But as I discovered more about him, some of his comments and behaviors made it easy to imagine that he likely could have cheated on his wife. Whether I was right or wrong probably isn't as important as all the little clues that gave me reason to hesitate. On the other hand, one gentleman I met confessed to infidelity, but was also able and willing to name the hurt and damage it caused within his family. I appreciated that self-awareness. The way a man narrates the challenges and difficult seasons of his past matters.

Response: Notice the ways a man describes the missteps and blunders from his past. If you suspect a lack of integrity, explore further.

A MAN DISPARAGES HIS FORMER PARTNER.

When I spoke on the phone with Bryan, he ranted, "My ex is a real nut job. I mean, totally psycho! Even her family thinks so. I mean, she is *really* messed up."

Maybe she was. Maybe she wasn't. I have no way of knowing. What mattered more to me than the mental health of Bryan's former spouse was the anger and unkindness I heard in his voice.

In the end, it doesn't matter if a particular woman—whom you really don't know and who is not there to give her perspective—was bitter or pleasant, a thrifty spender or a shopaholic, a hoarder or a minimalist. No matter what this man experienced with his previous partner, he has a choice about the way he frames who she is—both for himself and for others. A man's description about a woman from his past reveals more about him than it does about her.

One man told me that his wife had had an affair. And although he had not cheated on her, he admitted to me that he believed he was also partially culpable for the demise of their marriage. Mad respect for that guy.

When a widower shared about his ongoing love for the wife he lost, I realized that when he said he probably wasn't yet ready to date, he was *right*. But I also appreciated the strains of love, adoration, and gratitude I heard in his voice.

Because the majority of men whom we women meet in our later years have been married at least once, don't miss the opportunity to ask a man about his former spouse.

"Tell me something about the woman to whom you were married."

"I'm curious why your marriage didn't work out."

"What is it that you appreciated most about your for-mer wife?"

It can be tricky. I get that. But learning about a man's former relationships provides a valuable window into who he is.

Response: Steer clear of men who use their online real estate to speak ill of a former partner.

A MAN IS STRAIGHT-UP FOUL.

This one probably doesn't need to even be mentioned, but here I go: if a man doesn't have the good common sense to hide his ugly side until the fifth or sixth date, pass him by.

I'm thinking especially of these winners:

"Hit me up if you want to get high and then lie to your loved ones about it later."

"I only smoke if we are drinking a lot."

"You're so b-l-e-e-p-i-n-g hot! I just want to . . ." (I'll let you use your imagination.)

"I like the mountains and drinking. I am the head of any relationship. My needs come first. I like being in charge most of the time. I am a leader among men."

These have been cut and pasted, people. Cut and pasted.

Response: Avoid men who unabashedly tout their dark side.

A MAN POSTS A PICTURE WITH HIS CURRENT LIVING, LEGAL WIFE.

I wish this red flag was fictional. It's not.

Response: Run away. Quickly.

A MAN BOMBS YOU WITH INTEREST AND ATTENTION.

You might be thinking that being showered with affection sounds awesome. And you'd be right. When you believe you have a genuinely special connection with someone, it feels fantastic. But Dr. Suzanne Degges-White warns, "There's a saying that if something seems too good to be true, it probably is."[2]

On our first phone call, when Ike said he wanted me to meet his sister, a teeny part of me knew it felt a bit too quick. I felt the same when he added that his buddy from college would love me. And, on the same call, when he suggested a hysterical couples Halloween costume we could wear, I giggled, even though common sense told me it hinted at a future we may or may not end up having together. When he told me the funny question to ask his dad to really get him talking, I wasn't sure what to say. And when I shared a vulnerable piece of my story and he suggested we could spend the next forty years unpacking it, I did the age math and figured it was technically possible we could get that many years in together before the grave. But here's the rub: Ike said these words—and so many more fabulous ones—in the first, and only, week that we knew each other!

Dr. Degges-White describes what's known as "love bombing," saying, "When a relationship moves too fast—or one partner tries to push it too forcefully—it's essential that you call your partner on it, and let him or her know how you feel. . . . If a partner won't listen to your protestations and just tries to excuse away the smothering behavior, that's a sign that there's only likely to be less freedom and more manipulation in the future if you stay together."[3]

Response: As the good doctor suggests, have a conversation. You may not want to, but the way it unfolds will give you the insight you need to know whether to hit the gas or pump the brakes.

Here's the thing, friend: I completely understand how it can be tempting to overlook any of these warning signs if a fellow has a particularly attractive feature. For instance, the man who helps at-risk youth is my kryptonite. Truly, he could admit a penchant for bludgeoning freckled, blue-eyed, middle-aged moms of teenagers, and I'd be like, "Let me think this over for a sec . . . because he helps at-risk youth . . ."

If you're struggling to use your best judgment, ask yourself, "Would I want my best girlfriend, whom I love and protect, to go out with this guy?" If your gut says no, you have your answer. Trust your instincts and pump the brakes when you see a red flag.

In all moments, keep your eyes open and give yourself the gift of self-care.

PEOPLE LIE

HuffPost reports that 53 percent of online daters fabricate all or part of their profiles.[4] Yikes. Women lie about how many years we've been alive and men lie about income or success at work.[5] Though I have no hard evidence, I'm cautious about believing this fellow I came across: "Ive saved n the us marines. I am single educated with a phd doctrant n psychology." (Did he *really* earn a doctrant?) Also, some of the men using online dating sites are already married. Statistics vary, but even *one* is too many. Be cautious.

eighteen

PRACTICING SELF-CARE WHILE DATING

Two Women Open Up and Break It Down

Wise women learn how to practice self-care
from those who have gone before us.

When Jesus sent his disciples out into the wild, he coached them, "Behold, I send you forth as sheep in the midst of wolves: be ye therefore wise as serpents, and harmless as doves" (Matt. 10:16 KJV). Because he wanted his friends to *survive* in the wilderness, Jesus told them that they'd need to be pretty smart about it. And this is exactly how I send my sweet sheepish friends into the world of online dating. Because . . . wolves.

If you're like me, you need a guide to coach you in the ways of the wilderness. And that's why I wanted to ask two savvy friends to share with us from their dating experience. These dating savants, two black women, exercise both wisdom and the ability to practice self-care. To my ear, their experience dating as women of color equips all of us to keep our eyes open to some of the quiet subtleties of online dating.

Olivia names what is unique about dating as a woman of color, explaining, "The challenges for women of color are different. While many men are willing to date white women, fewer men—of a variety of races—are open to dating women of color. It's frustrating." Marie-Gabrielle adds, "You have to approach it with discernment and with a bit more skepticism."

Both women noticed that some black men explicitly announce in their profiles that they prefer women of another race, such as white or Asian or Latina. Some men, of all races, will use code by saying things like "race is not an issue for me" or "I date everyone" to subtly signal a preference to date women outside of their own race. Now you know.

A study of heterosexual male OkCupid users exposed what Olivia and Marie-Gabrielle already knew about race and attraction:

1. Non-black men were less likely to start conversations with black women.
2. Black men showed little racial preference either way.[1]

What I was most eager to learn from Olivia and Marie-Gabrielle was what they would want other women to know about dating online as a woman of color. If you're not a woman of color, listen for the ways their serpentine wisdom resonates with your own experience. Here's what they shared:

1. **Some dating sites have greater racial diversity than others.** If you're interested in dating a man of color, some sites will make that easier than others. Both Olivia and Marie-Gabrielle agree that it is easier to find users who are men of color on Tinder, Match, and OkCupid. Conversely, they name Bumble, Hinge, and Coffee Meets Bagel as being pretty *white*.

2. **Some men want to experiment dating someone they consider "exotic."** Some men, often white ones, have heard rumors about what it is like to be with a woman of another race, so they're interested in "trying" it. These men may be more interested in using you, in ways that may or may not include sex, than in truly getting to know who you are.

3. **Some men will be overly eager for you to know that they are down with your race.** Some men, often white ones, may go out of their way to let you know that they have experience with women of other races. Or they'll stumble over themselves trying to communicate that they're woke. If it feels awkward to you, it's because it is. Red flag.

4. **Some men will struggle more than others to fully understand your experience as a woman of color.** While no one besides another woman of color who shares a very similar experience of the world as you will be able to understand your experience intimately, some men will find understanding your experience to be *more* of a challenge than others. It will be up to you to decide how much of your energy you want to spend translating your world for a

man with a vastly different life experience. If he has lots of good qualities, you may decide to spend the energy it takes to teach him. And if it's more emotionally taxing than life-giving to be with him, you may decide it's not worth it.

5. **None of us live in isolation, including the men we date. They have family and friends.** As you get to know a man of a different race, you'll inevitably spend time with his family and friends. In those environments, notice which one of you is carrying the burden of dealing with any ignorance or microaggressions. If you have to use a lot of energy calling them out, you will be exhausted. But if he takes the initiative to check and educate them, you may be willing to put up with it.

6. **Notice cues that signal whether a man has experience interacting with people outside of his race.** If a man has photographs showing him in multicultural settings, it might be fair to assume that you will not be the first person of color with whom he's interacted. Conversely, Olivia and Marie-Gabrielle note that if you see a white man who's pretty politically and religiously conservative, and who only has pictures with his white golfing buddies, you may want to be more cautious. These may be subtle cues both that you may not be selected, and also that you might need to practice self-protection if you are.

7. **A woman of color holding a position of power can be an intimidating combination for some men.** All women who hold positions of power, privilege, or prestige—doctors, lawyers, executives, leaders, etc.—have to decide how they will "package" themselves in their profiles. For example,

rather than touting her professional accomplishments, Marie-Gabrielle writes in her profile that she enjoys "cooking." While it's *true*, she's also aware that by dialing back her undeniable glory and power, she is catering to the ego of men who could be threatened by all she is. Both women note that some men will shy away from the challenge of navigating the tricky convergence of race, gender, and power.

Marie-Gabrielle and Olivia share these noticings with sweet sheep like you and me, with the protective heart of the wise big sister who wants to help you avoid learning life lessons the hard way.

But they're also quick to note that there are men of all races, including white men, who would make great partners. Marie-Gabrielle was quick to affirm, "There are genuine white men out there. I've dated white men who are interested in who I am. That's important. I dated one for a while who cared deeply for me."

As we say in the world of improv, "Yes, *and* . . ." Yes, there will be men of all races in the dating pool who have the capacity to love you. *And*—equally, if not more importantly—practicing self-care means that you need to be wise and careful as you date.

nineteen

SUSPICION, SMARTS, AND SAFETY

Catfish Cautions

You can choose to be smart and safe
about men you're meeting.

The salon where I get my hair cut is that iconic kind of beauty shop where, on a good day, soulful ladies sit around for hours gabbing about nothing and everything. Though it only occurs to me to get my hair cut about once a year, I'll still stop in regularly to say happy birthday to Carla, or to gush over a picture of Tamika's new baby, or to admire Lourdes's amazing rainbow hair. After I say hey to Cherrie as she's smoothing someone's locks, I turn toward Tamika and Carla, who look up from whatever heads they're attending to. Predictably, they chime "Margot!" in unison, as if they're truly happy to see me. (If you watched the sitcom *Cheers* in the eighties, then you can imagine this feels just like when Norm walks into the bar and is greeted with an enthusiastic, "Norm!")

So imagine how thrilled I was, during my annual scheduled visit, to scoot into Carla's chair and realize that the ladies were already talking about *online dating*. I quickly figured out that Tamika and Carla had a shared acquaintance who'd gotten suckered by some guy online. This woman I'll call Monique had been dating a guy she really liked. In fact, Bo was so awesome that he was planning to buy her a home. So when an unexpected situation came up for Bo and he needed quick cash, it was natural for Monique to lend him the money.

And then Bo vanished.

Monique had been catfished—lured into a relationship by someone who was not who he appeared to be.

Until that trip to TLC Salon, I always assumed that the people who got hoodwinked were the ones who sent money to an acquaintance frantically emailing that he was "stuck overseas" or who thoughtlessly shared their banking details over the phone. I wanted to believe that I could never be fooled like that.

But . . . *Monique*. I've thought of her often. If I was in a relationship with someone I believed truly cared about me, with whom I was building a financially solid future, I could imagine wanting to be that generous. Suddenly it was easy to see how Monique had gotten tangled up in Bo's twisty web.

A few weeks later, when I met my friend Glory for lunch at California Pizza Kitchen, she shared that there were lots of guys online who'd tried to catfish her, presumably because she was a successful business owner. Because she really is the Beyoncé of business, I guess they figured she was loaded. Honestly, if I was an unethical creepy catfishing dude, I would totally choose Glory. As I gobbled up my Margherita pizza, it slowly dawned on me that no one online had even made the effort to catfish me. My profile says I'm a "writer," which I'm sure is just about as alluring to a catfisher as "starving artist." So suddenly I was feeling a little miffed to have not been catfished. But eventually I let it go. Because I'm grown.

But the story's not over. Because one guy out there had somehow not gotten the message that I wasn't worth catfishing.

The week before Christmas I had connected with an architect who lived just two states away in Georgia. He'd spent the first eighteen years of his life in Norway before moving to the United States after his parents died. He had a son who lived in California and who was visiting him in Georgia for the holidays, along with his aunt and uncle. And this gentleman was busy preparing a presentation to bid on a big job. Clearly, his backstory had been carefully constructed.

For reasons I still can't quite pinpoint, I didn't get overly invested in this dreamy guy the way I'm apt to do. Sometimes the language he used for his faith rubbed me the wrong way; it sounded overspiritualized. I got no indication that he had a community of support or a network of friends. And when we spoke on the phone, I got a little freaked out by what presumably was a Norwegian accent. I don't know if it was or not. To my untrained ear, he sounded more like the weaselly French archnemesis of Ricky Bobby in *Talladega Nights* than the Swedish chef on the Muppets—who is my only culturally inappropriate reference point to know what someone from Norway might sound like. For whatever fortuitous reason, something inside me was taking it slow, exercising caution with this guy.

We were actually discussing the possibility of meeting up at some point, after he knocked out the big presentation, when a girlfriend of mine poked her nose into my business. Protective, naturally suspicious, Lizbeth wanted to make sure this guy was on the up and up. Honestly, I didn't give her much intel at all, but when I mentioned that he only had two Facebook friends, all her warning bells started chiming. In the blink of an eye she knew he wasn't real. And once she said it, I knew that Lizbeth was probably right. In retrospect, all the signs were there. Lizbeth knew what I did not: proceeding with suspicion is safe and smart.

Although his eHarmony profile said "Thomas," he signed his first text to me as "Jason." When I asked about the discrepancy, he let me know that people called him by his middle name, Jason. Fine. Whatever.

When I returned to peek at his profile on eHarmony after we'd exchanged phone numbers, it was gone. Fair. People take breaks from online dating when they've just met somebody who's awesome.

When I googled the name of this accomplished professional, the only architect with that name was someone half Thomas-Jason's age who was practicing on the West Coast.

When I searched on LinkedIn, there was no record of Thomas-Jason.

Then I promptly let him know I was done.

Is there a chance that I was wrong? Sure, I'm willing to entertain the possibility that there was a teeny-weeny miniscule chance. But I wasn't willing to take that risk. I still don't understand what he was hoping to gain with the ruse. I understand that some people catfish successful women like Glory in the hopes of financial gain, but I'm not entirely clear about the other reasons.

One study claims that most catfishers go fishin' for revenge, or due to loneliness, or because of boredom.[1] (Really? Get a better hobby.) I don't know what Thomas-Jason's excuse was, but I said good riddance! You may have tricked me, Thomas-Jason, but you didn't trick my savvy friend Lizbeth!

Here is what I recommend when communicating with matches:

BE SUSPICIOUS

Business Insider reports that one out of ten online profiles is fake—more often on free sites than on paid ones.[2] Exercise caution as you're getting to know *anyone* online. In fact, if you share no common acquaintances with someone, it's not the worst idea in the world to assume that person is guilty until proven innocent. I mean that in the most loving way, of course.

BE SMART

Do a little research on the guy you're getting to know. When I finally asked one guy his last name, I stumbled upon his mug shot online. I met another man who claimed that he didn't google women he met online. When I suggested it, he made it seem as if it was a *really* dumb idea. It made more sense after I googled him and found the paparazzi pictures of him exiting the courthouse during a high-profile criminal trial.

BE SAFE ONLINE

You already know all the things about being safe. Protect your personal information. Don't give out your address. Don't share too much too quickly. Don't share photos you don't want shared with others.

BE SAFE IN PERSON

Arrange to meet in a public place. Plan your own transportation. Let a friend know where you'll be.

BE SHARING

Two heads are always better than one. If you have a girlfriend who's willing to listen, loop her in on your dating fiestas and fiascos. Sometimes she'll catch something that you've missed.

Just as we make choices to stay physically safe while dating, one of the ways we keep ourselves emotionally safe is by releasing those who are unable to see who we really are.

I DID IT SO YOU DON'T HAVE TO

"I Didn't Do My Research"

While online friendships usually begin on a first-name basis, once you feel comfortable with someone, it's fair game to ask his last name so you can google him or search for him on social media. Because you most likely know what he looks like, this shouldn't be too difficult.

If he has a very common name, it might take a little more creativity. And while you can't trust everything you read online, and you certainly can't presume to know how a man's past has shaped the man he is today, you can usually learn *something* about who a man is.

- **Google him.** Use first name, last name, city, employment. See what you can discover.
- **Find him on Facebook or other social media platforms.** Whatever he posts will give you insight into who he is. But, possibly even more significant, what do others have to say to him and about him? Have his children tagged him in family posts? What comments have friends left?
- **Find him on LinkedIn.** Yeah, work life might not be fascinating, but it could be a helpful clue to whether he does or does not exist.
- **Do a criminal background check.** Without my knowledge or permission, my friend Emily did a criminal background check on someone of whom I was quite fond. What she found helped me understand some weird things he'd said on the phone about college panty raids. While it wasn't a deal breaker, it was useful information to factor into the whole equation.
- **Use your cell phone.** If you have a landline, that phone number can be linked to your address. So for safety's sake, begin conversations with someone on your cell until you know him better.
- **Drive yourself.** Until you know someone well, use your own transportation to meet up.

twenty

WHEN OUR CULTURE CAN'T SEE US CLEARLY

Honoring Our Own Value

Our inherent value can never be determined
by the way others do or do not see us.

My friend Nicole, the author of *Fat and Faithful: Learning to Love Our Bodies, Our Neighbors, and Ourselves*, has experience dating as a woman who is fat. (Did I just struggle to type the *f* word, the one that describes women's bodies as being larger than average? Yeah, I did. But I forced myself to do it because it's the word Nicole uses and I *wisely* take all my cues about larger women from her.)

Without knowing what number you see when you glance down at the bathroom scale, or the one you hear the nurse in the doctor's office announcing in a voice that always seems way too loud, there's no doubt in my mind that something from Nicole's experience is going to resonate with your own.

Because, as girls, a lot of us wondered if we'd find "the one."

We wondered if we'd be seen for who we are.

Today we are committed to living rich, beautiful lives as single women.

And we know, in our deep places, that while our bodies are an important part of who we are, we are also so much more.

Because Nicole is convinced of her undeniable worth as a woman who's created in God's image, which I believe is contagious, I want you to get infected by her certainty.

So sit down, get comfy, and join us as we chat.

Margot: Growing up, as a girl who was fat, what did you believe about your future potential to be desired by a man as a potential wife?

Nicole: I was convinced that it would be difficult to find someone who would want to marry me, but I believed that non-Christian men would outright ignore me because of my fat body, as I was taught they only cared about sex. I desperately hoped and believed that Christian men, or at least the one "right" Christian man, would see my "inner beauty" and be okay with my body. I never in my wildest imaginations thought anyone would be physically attracted to me.

Margot: What changed?

Nicole: Experience proved everything wrong. I had my

149

first date at twenty and ended up in a relationship that wasn't great, as I just assumed the first person to express interest had to be "the one" because who else would want me? After that relationship ended, I went into the online dating game. I quickly saw the pattern: Christian men weren't interested, and non-Christian men were much more willing to see me as a full person and were attracted to the full picture of who I am. And many other fat women share experiences similar to mine.

Margot: Wait, let's not zip past that. Why do you think that is?

Nicole: My best guess is that Christian men are taught that they are "poet warriors" who will defend and rescue a "captivating" woman. "Righteous fox" was a common descriptor of pastor wives back in the day. It's like they deserve a pretty wife if they are a "godly leader." And then the church does nothing to critique cultural beauty norms.

Margot: How do you understand your identity now, as a woman who is entirely worthy of attention and love from men?

Nicole: I am a woman who has value, regardless of what men or anyone else find attractive about me. Yes, I want to have a partner who will support me in all the ways and who will delight in me in all the ways partners and spouses delight in each other, but at thirty-six I've learned that's not a mandatory requirement for a full life. The opposite of loneliness is not marriage, but community. Community can provide so much of what we look for in a partner: support, encouragement, joining in on important work and holiday memories.

Margot: A friend of mine has had a relatively good experience on sites designed for men who are attracted to fat women, and says it just makes "fat" a nonissue. Your thoughts?

Nicole: They seem to cater to men who want to fetishize fat women. I am not a fan.

Margot: Any tips on that, in general?

Nicole: Know the difference between someone interested in you and someone who is fetishizing you. Men can be naturally attracted to fat women and *not* fetishize that attraction. Just like we can be attracted to people with brown hair and not fetishize that attraction. Pay attention and be safe. Trust your gut. If you are looking for a relationship, you deserve someone who values your entire self.

Margot: I know you've been brave recently as you've been doing some online dating. How's that been?

Nicole: I've dated more this year than the rest of my life because I told myself to take chances. I'm actually surprised at how often I've gone on dates; I've got bad first-date stories and stood-up stories and all kinds of stuff now. Nothing great or lasting, but I'm glad I'm trying. I've become braver and more sure of what I want, and don't want, this year. It's been a beneficial endeavor regardless.

Margot: What do you want to say to a woman who's fat and considering online dating?

Nicole: My biggest tip for other fat women in online dating is to not hide yourself. Camera angles can do wonders, but don't hide behind them. Post pictures of yourself you love and include both close-up selfies and full-body shots. Don't apologize for yourself. Describe your victories and joys and quirks, not your flaws and insecurities. Take chances and interrogate your resistance to people, but don't settle. You don't have to accept the first thing that comes along out of fear that there might not be another. Listen to your gut. Consult your community when red flags pop up and run if they tell you to run. You are enough and you are not too much.

Margot: Huge thanks to you, Nicole. We're nourished by your insights.

Reader girl, were you infected by Nicole's confidence in your own undeniable God-given value and lovability? I was.

WEATHERING THE JOURNEY

The root choice is to trust at all times that God is with you and will give you what you most need.

—*Henri Nouwen*

twenty-one

RESILIENCE

Bumps, Bruises, and Bouncing Back

The steadfast love of God is sturdier
than the trials you will face.

"Margot, that wasn't a good lead-in."

Yes, this is feedback on my writing.

No, it's not from an English professor or a writing-group critique partner. It's from a guy online who didn't like the message I'd sent him.

I racked my brain for what I'd done wrong.

Margot, did you send another explicit and inappropriate selfie?

Did you use profanity in that first message?

Girl, did you use off-color humor again?

No, none of those things.

I'd begun by announcing, "I want to say hey,"—which is exactly what we say here in North Carolina—"because you seem awesome." *I mean, who doesn't want to get that message?* The thumbs-up emoji I got right back made me think we were in agreement that someone awesome had patiently received my awkward greeting.

So I felt like the door was open for us to get to know one another.

Which is why I went with, "I think I read that you're a student now . . . what were you up to before that?"

To my ear, it was a fair question. But George didn't think so.

"Good morning. Why are you asking me that? Margot, that wasn't a good lead-in."

My face flushed hot with shame. Regret. Embarrassment.

A little eight-inch-tall devil on my right shoulder started to get heated with a little animated angel on my left one. They looked like stereotypical cartoon versions of me, one fiercely fiery and the other wholly holy.

> **Devil Margot:** Um, are you kidding me right now? You just screwed up your courage to let this joker know he's fantastic, and he's giving you lessons in etiquette?!

That red-tailed, pitchfork-holding gal really made a good point. But so did her holy counterpart, speaking calmly into my other ear.

> **Angel Margot:** Margot, you know how that polite Pastor Phil begins all of his emails and texts to you, no matter how mundane, with a polite greeting? Maybe that's how all decent people are supposed to communicate with one another. Maybe only animals don't begin with

a courteous, "Top of the morning to you, stranger!"

Devil Margot: This isn't a networking brunch in Dublin. It's the freakin' internet, home of TBH, LOL, and LMAO. This is how 99.99 percent of the people who use it communicate.

Angel Margot: But there's no reason not to be thoughtful, polite, and respectful. You really should have known better.

Back and forth they went, debating what seemed to be my deal-breaking blunder.

In the end I decided I'd blown it and just let it go. Because he really did seem awesome, I might have tried harder had he been local. But I certainly didn't need to force something cross-country that was already destined for inherent difficulty.

That day whenever I thought about the app, or my enthusiastic message, or words, I felt ashamed. I didn't really think that I'd done anything so horribly wrong, but I recognized that flushed feeling that I didn't like as shame.

I asked for this.

I did this on purpose.

Why am I doing this?

Like all of the other bruises, bumps, and scrapes on the dating journey, this one made me question why I would willingly make myself vulnerable to all the feelings that one is bound to experience in the absurd process of trying to meet and get to know, and ideally get to like and love, someone online.

After getting dumped by a guy I liked named Mel, I narrated the disappointing debacle to a friend of mine, Emily, who'd been traveling with me over the course of the whole journey with him.

Emily is a therapist who specializes in working with adolescents. So, as a middle-aged woman trying to date, I sort of hit the friend jackpot with her. When I recounted how the dumping unfolded, I bravely narrated it for her by saying that I had learned a lot and I was better because of it, blah blah blah. I really made it sound like *I* was the big winner.

The next day I got a message from Emily saying, "You have the healthiest ego of anyone ever."

For a few hours, I felt really happy and proud about that compliment. Then it dawned on me that it was probably shrink speak for, "The defenses that keep you from crumbling into a pile of dust, the way any normally functioning woman would and *should* under the same circumstances, are quite formidable."

LOL.

While I might be an extreme case, with my overly robust sense of self-worth, I really do believe that we have the choice to assign meaning to our own experiences. And while the hiss of the voice that lies will seize every opportunity to persuade us that we are not enough, the voice that cannot lie confirms what is most true about you and about me:

- *You are worth knowing.*
- *You are worth loving.*
- *You are enough.*

Being rejected for any reason hurts. Whether it's being chastised for reasons that aren't clear or being rebuffed for reasons that are far more personal, rejection stings. This journey is fraught with disappointments, hurts, and rejections. And yet, for most of us, experiencing pain on the dating journey is unavoidable.

Although I wouldn't have chosen some of the hurts I've endured in this dating process, I can see the ways I am growing through them. I'm becoming smarter about reading the signs. I'm releasing control and trusting in God. I'm protecting my heart in the best way. But hurt is still hurt.

Human love fails. It just does. Even if you or I were to find our Mr. Right—I mean a really emotionally healthy, godly man—he would still not be equipped to love perfectly. Nor was he made to.

Thankfully, there is One whose love does not fail.

Hear me: I don't mean this in any fluffy, trite, "even if people don't love you, God loves you" kind of way. Never. Blech. The steadfastness and reliability of God's unflagging love for you is weighty, and solid, and more real and enduring than any human experience. It doesn't mean that God's love is a substitute for the human love you're missing. It means that God's abiding love is always with you: as you're browsing through profiles, when you get ghosted, and over all the months and years when finding someone is taking much, much longer than you'd prefer. In every moment, God's love abides with you.

If you've felt beat up in this process, I am so sorry. And I'm also very confident that our gracious Father is close to you, longing to comfort you in your sadness. Sometimes that comfort will come through the fierce tribe of women God has given you. Sometimes it may be a phrase from Scripture that you recognize to be truer than the naughty voice of the enemy. And sometimes it might be as simple as closing your eyes and visualizing the Lord's promised nearness to the brokenhearted.

Sister, you are not alone.

In fact, I believe that you are even equipped to survive and thrive if a man never responds to you at all.

twenty-two

WHEN HE DOESN'T RESPOND

Why the Story You Make Up Matters

The negative and positive feelings we experience are driven
by the story we tell ourselves about our experience.

Let's say a girlfriend and I are supposed to meet each other at
the movies, but I'm running late. My cell phone is dead, so my
girlfriend is in the dark. In all the ways. Ten minutes after the
movie starts, I clumsily step over seven moviegoers in her row
who showed up on time, and as I drop into my sticky plush red
seat, I have no idea how she'll react.

Maybe she snaps at me for being so rude.

Or she might be really bummed out if she believes that my
tardiness indicated a lack of love for her.

Or perhaps she is genuinely anxious and concerned about
me, wondering if I'm okay or if I've been in an accident.

Same event, three different reactions. And each of them hinges on the meaning, or the *story*, that she has attached to the fact that I was late.

The way we think about an event—the meaning we assign to it—determines the way we feel about it.

If she's thinking, "Margot is so inconsiderate," she'll probably feel angry.

If she's thinking, "Margot doesn't care about our relationship," she might feel sad.

And if she's thinking, "Margot could have been hit by a bus," she could feel fearful.

If her feelings are big ones, she might not even notice she's having any of those thoughts—even though the thought is the whole reason for the feeling that's welled up inside of her!

When we're unaware of the story we assign to an event, we can be bullied by our feelings. So the big win is to be able to notice the thoughts we're having, or the story we're telling ourselves, about a certain event. When we notice the way we're interpreting our experience, we don't have to be bossed around by our feelings because we're free to choose a new story.

When I arrive late to the theater—whispering excitedly about all the cheap dollar-store candy I have stuffed in my pockets and socks and all the places—my girlfriend has the opportunity to expose the story she's made up about my absence, to check in and see how real it is.

My friend might say, "The story I make up is that you could have called to let me know you were running late, but you didn't."

Or she might confess, "I make up that whatever you were doing was more important than me."

Or, finally exhaling, she might tell me, "The thought in my head was that you were in an accident and died."

When she's able to notice and name the story in her head, she doesn't have to be bossed around by anger or sadness or fear.

Isn't that sort of fantastic?

Apologetic and kind, I can offer another story that is truer than any of the three that might have caused her distress.

"I'm so sorry I'm late. I wanted to call and let you know I'd stopped by the dollar store to get your favorite candy—which, by the way, is melting in my bra right now—but my phone died. I apologize for making you wait."

If she's willing, my friend can replace the story that is causing her distress with one that is truer.

The reason I bring this up is because the experience of waiting for a man to reply to a message you've sent online is a bit like this. In many ways it's *exactly* like this.

Let's say you messaged a guy at 7 p.m. and when you wake up the next morning you've still not heard from him. The feeling you'll experience about this guy not responding to your message depends on the story you tell yourself about why he didn't respond.

If you're like me and have developed pretty robust emotional defense mechanisms, you could think, *He read my message and actually loved it. And me. But he just had a first date with another woman. He probably secretly hopes it doesn't work out with her, because he loved my profile so much.* (Truly, what is in my head to protect me from getting hurt is nothing short of sheer wizardry.)

Or, when you don't hear back from him, you may reason, *He hasn't read my message. He's a busy attorney and probably can't be bothered by dating app notifications dinging on his phone all day. So he might not even read my message until the weekend, if ever. Because if he'd read it, I'm pretty sure he would have responded.*

Or you might figure, *He read my message and something*

signaled to him we weren't a match. Maybe he's allergic to my horrible cat. Whatever. His loss.

Or you might say to yourself, *He read my message, looked at my profile, and thought I was a loser.*

When someone doesn't respond to a message you've sent—or even when they respond to say that they're not interested—you don't have to be bullied by your feelings. In fact, the way you navigate the entire dating process is up to you. If you think that you're a loser who is probably going to be rejected, each unreturned message is going to feel like you're being knocked down by a huge wave at the beach. But if you have decided that you are an amazing woman with so much to offer the right person, then disappointments and even flat-out rejections can roll past you like a gentle wave.

I know it can be hard not to take it personally when you don't receive a reply from a guy you dig. But it's not necessarily about you. (Well, if you've threatened to murder his dog if he doesn't reply, it may be about you.) I want you to hear that you have no idea what's happening inside the person who's peeking at your photos, reading your profile, or typing you messages. You don't know if he's been hurt and is afraid of commitment. You don't know if an innocent mention triggered something difficult inside him. You don't know if he had a really mean third-grade teacher who had the same name as you. You just don't know. So I want to encourage you to hold those interactions lightly, and cling tightly to what is most true: you are acceptable; you are beloved; you are cherished. Notice the story you tell yourself about disappointments and rejections.

While I'm confident that you have everything you need for this journey, sometimes it is longer and more grueling than we might choose. Graciously, God equips you to wait with patience and courage.

twenty-three

LONELINESS

When the Wait Is Longer Than We'd Like

When you acknowledge and feel your loneliness,
trusting God, you can move through it.

"How ya doing?" a friend asked as we were chatting over the snack table at a stupid Sunday afternoon homeowner's meeting.

Had she been anyone else, I would have dodged the question, randomly remarking, "The weather is beautiful! How are you?"

But she wasn't anyone else. She was Susan. And Susan's on my squad.

"Well," I reported, without my signature pep, "the loneliness came on Friday, as usual. Because it's the weekend."

She knows how this can happen when the weekend comes.

Then I added, "And today I was too sad to skate."

That last sentence is when her eyes bugged out of her head.

Too sad to roller-skate on a weekend? She understood immediately that what I was experiencing was a pretty seismic sadness.

It's been six years since my husband left our home. Not that anyone's keeping track, but he's married and I'm alone. (Okay, maybe I'm keeping track.) In fact, just three months after moving out of the home we shared with our children, my ex-husband met the person who would become his spouse. So some days I wonder if God might have fallen asleep on the job.

Admitting my loneliness to a friend like Susan can feel a little embarrassing, even though I know it shouldn't. So I'll dodge that discomfort, or create extra discomfort for the listener, in all kinds of ways.

If someone asks me how I'm doing, I might modify an honest explanation by admitting only that "I'm man-lonely." Then I leave the listener to imagine whatever creepy thing I might mean by that.

Or I'll admit that I'm lonely, but then quickly comfort the other by adding, "I mean, it's sort of baffling, because I have this awesome life. I have this rich community, and friends I spend time with, and all these awesome people who love me."

But if I'm brave, I'll leave it at the truth: *I'm lonely.*

It's always a little hard to spit out.

And what's so sinister is that the voice that lies capitalizes on that loneliness and hisses quietly in my ear, "You shouldn't be lonely."

And though the exhortation almost sounds benign, it's not at all. Because that tricky voice is insinuating that there's something wrong with me, or with you, for feeling lonely. It hints that we are to blame. The deceiver quietly suggests that I am, or you are, *responsible* for our loneliness.

It's uncomfortable to stay with our loneliness. So on a lot of days, I do whatever I think will help me feel something other than the loneliness. I may eat a pint of Ben and Jerry's Half-Baked. Or I might watch a John Mulaney comedy special on Netflix. Wayward, I'll fill my mouth and eyes and ears with all manner of soothers.

Between my early twenties and early thirties, the difficult decade-long season when God was healing my heart from childhood hurts, I felt deep loneliness. It's when God gifted me with Henri Nouwen's beautiful little book *The Inner Voice of Love*. And while it's possible Henri Nouwen simply had no idea how effective either cookie-dough ice cream or John Mulaney could be at numbing painful feelings, he had a keen understanding of the impulse to escape loneliness.

Nouwen observed, "It is not easy to stay with your loneliness. The temptation is to nurse your pain or escape into fantasies about people who will take it away." Okay, he *really* gets it. Then Nouwen continued, "But when you can acknowledge your loneliness in a safe, contained place, you make your pain available for God's healing."[1]

What he's saying is that when we use all of our numbing soothers to avoid pain, it stays with us. If we want for God to fill and heal our loneliness, we must *allow* it rather than avoid it. Clearly, it's all very counterintuitive.

Nouwen exhorted, "God does not want your loneliness. Got wants to touch you in a way that permanently fills your deepest need. You have to own your loneliness and trust that it will not always be there."[2] For loneliness to pass, we have to *own* it first. Beloved, not only is there no shame in loneliness, but when we offer it to the Lord, God graciously receives and redeems it.

I know this may be hard to believe, but the numbing effects of the ice cream and the Netflix comedy special did not last long. (Somehow this *always* surprises me.) And when the ineffective substitutes were revealed as counterfeits, I got up with the One who loves me. Face-to-face with God, I heard three things:

1. I am with you and for you.
2. I redeem.
3. I long to be gracious.

And in my spirit, I knew each one to be true.

The first, that God is with me and for me, are words that God spoke to me about fifteen years ago, during that precious season of healing, to which I have clung ever since.

The second awareness is the sense that God redeems. I don't know exactly what God's redemption in my life will look like next, but I do know that I have experienced God's creativity in the unlikely ways he has redeemed the most difficult situations in my life.

And, finally, I heard the beautiful assurance spoken in Isaiah 30:18, "Yet the LORD longs to be gracious to you; therefore he will rise up to show you compassion. For the LORD is a God of justice. Blessed are all who wait for him!" God *longs* to be gracious. I was hungry to experience God's graciousness and compassion. But truth be told, I was not a big fan of that last part. The *waiting*. Like a petulant child, I'd much prefer not to wait.

I remember clearly that September soccer day when a switch flipped inside me and I was finally ready to date. Though I had no idea at the time, I can see now that I was probably not as realistic as I should have been about the length of time it would take to lock down a man. Basically, I had no inkling that I might need to wait.

So you can imagine my dismay when I didn't meet Prince Charming that first day. Or the first week. Or the first month. Or the first year. (Please, Jesus, don't let me ever have to add "first decade.") And although the fact that I had to wait, and am still waiting, should not have come as a surprise to me, or anyone who's been alive more than thirteen years, somehow it did. Because of my awesome karma. And my magical thinking.

That I am still waiting, a few years into this journey, surprises me most days. Yet during the few fleeting moments when I actually am grounded in reality, I remember I'm not alone. One friend of mine has been waiting five years. Another, fifty-five years.

Waiting is an integral part of the dating journey. And while I wish I could say that with all the practice I've become some kind of Zen-Yoda master at patience, I've actually never been worse at waiting than I have during this season I've been waiting on God to pony up. I am more impatient than ever.

Because the wait feels lonely.

Ella is a friend of mine who's been single for about fifteen years. And when I asked about her singleness, she explained that a few times a year she'll feel lonely, tell God about it, have a good cry, and then get back to living. Something about her posture toward loneliness seemed so right. First, I was grateful that she was willing to be vulnerable enough to say it out loud. It would have been much easier for her to answer, "The weather is beautiful! How are you?" So thank you, Ella. But I also thought that the practice of noticing the loneliness, feeling it, and letting it pass, was therapeutic genius. According to my understanding, this is how feelings work. When we resist our negative feelings, they stay; when we feel our negative feelings, they pass. Ella helped me remember that.

And I happen to be so *blessed*—insert eye-roll emoji here—that I've already had a chance to practice this lesson today! I shared with one friend by text and with another in our conversation on Facebook Messenger that because today is Friday, I'm feeling man-lonely. (You probably figured it out, but "man-lonely" isn't *entirely* creepy. It just means that I acknowledge I am surrounded and embraced by a community of people who love me fiercely, and who I love, but I am still itchy to find the right man with whom I can share my awesome life and awesome community.) So I did what Ella had modeled: I noticed my loneliness, shared it with God and a friend who cared, then returned to living.

I encourage you to practice this rhythm of releasing your loneliness to God.

Noticing our loneliness, and releasing it to God, is an act of trusting God. It might be as simple as noticing the loneliness inside you, in the presence of God, and then blowing it out in one big exhale as you type at your computer. Maybe you'll call a friend to let her know you're struggling with loneliness. Or it could be a simple prayer you speak aloud on your commute to the office: "God, I'm lonely. Trusting that you love me, I release it to you." Or perhaps, like that savvy Ella, you have a big ol' cry. Choose a practice that works for you and *use it*. And then notice what God does with your loneliness.

It really is counterintuitive, right? Too often we behave as if numbing or dodging our big emotions will spare us from feeling them. But the opposite is actually truer. When we own our loneliness, it no longer owns us. That's the big win.

At the end of his brief meditation, Nouwen challenged and

exhorted, "Dare to stay with your pain and trust God's promise to you."

Trust that God is with you and for you.

Trust that God redeems.

Trust that God longs to be gracious.

You can't get around your loneliness, and I hope you don't try. But with God's help, you can get through it.

And, graciously, when we practice exercising holy courage, the reward can be worth waiting for. It was for my friend, Van . . .

ALLOWING VERSUS RESISTING EXERCISE

There is a likely chance that in the course of the dating journey, you will experience feelings that are labeled by most as *negative*: sadness, anger, or fear. This is normal. And the magic secret about how to experience those feelings with less distress is pretty counterintuitive. When we resist negative feelings, they linger; when we accept negative feelings, they pass. This means that the big win is in allowing yourself to feel the feeling. Because feelings tell us something important about our experience, we can learn from them and then allow them to pass.

Visualize yourself wading in a gently flowing stream. The emotion you're feeling is a piece of bark, floating on top of the water and heading in your direction. Notice it, allow it, then watch it pass by. Try it.

twenty-four

ONE HAPPY ENDING

*When Exercising Courage While
Weathering the Journey Pays Off*

The courage required as we meet the
"wrong" people can pay off in the end.

When I began dating, my friend Vaneetha was one of the women my age who I knew had tried—and by "tried" I obviously mean "endured"—online dating. Van, who had polio as a child, was diagnosed in her forties with post-polio syndrome, which is a progressive illness that weakens the body. Not long after her diagnosis, her husband left her. After giving herself some time to heal, my amazing, brave friend gathered her courage and tried online dating. Her story is one of God's gracious provision. I asked her to share it to encourage us all. (Don't stop reading before the end. You'll thank me.)

Margot: As a girl, what did you believe about your future potential to be desired by a man as a potential wife?

Van: Being Indian, growing up in a white world, both my disability and my ethnicity made me feel like no one would really want me. I didn't date anybody until after college. Then, after my husband left, I tried online dating. It's hard for anyone to date online, to put yourself out there, but as a person with a disability it's not just me and my personality—*it's this other huge thing.* You feel like you're damaged goods. Why would they choose me when they could choose someone who's able-bodied?

Margot: Ouch. When you'd get discouraged, what helped?

Van: When I'd sink down, I'd just stay down until my friends would talk me out of it. God spoke truth to me, but it wasn't a quick fix. It was a combination of reading Scripture, going to friends, telling myself the truth, and even writing it out. It's telling yourself a different story about who you are.

Margot: So when you dated in your forties, how did men deal with your disability?

Van: If we were emailing and I told them about my disability, some of them emailed back and admitted they couldn't handle it. And they'd be done.

A guy I'd been talking to on the phone had been saying to me, "Aren't you feeling this unbelievable connection right now? I can't wait to meet you." After I told him that I'd had polio as a child and walked with a limp, I never heard from him after that.

I was always super nervous about meeting people in person. I handled it differently in different situations, but it was always really stressful for me. I went out with a guy who'd been a friend of mine, and I could tell he liked me. Then one night he took me out to dinner to tell me he couldn't date someone with a disability. Those things sting, and it's hard to get past them.

Margot: Ugh. That stinks. When would you say is the best time to mention your disability to a man?

Van: If you're going to meet someone in person, tell them ahead of time. But if you're just emailing, tell them when you start to feel like there's a connection. But you don't want to tell them so soon that they don't give you a chance.

Margot: So what do you want a woman with a disability who's considering online dating to know?

Van: I know this sounds crazy, but there is an advantage to having a disability—though I didn't see it when I was dating. You screen out all the weirdos and guys who are only there for a one-night stand. Only people with depth are willing to go out with someone who has a disability. That was my experience. Most of the guys I ended up dating had a level of depth that I appreciated. Women I know who are able-bodied and super-attractive get a lot of interest from very shallow people. I didn't have to deal with that.

Margot: That's the best silver lining I've ever heard. Those poor super-attractive women, I really pity them. Thank you, Van!

Whether or not we have a visible disability, the odds of finding the wonderful man God has for us aren't always in our favor. Across all the sites, most have a gender ratio that's pretty close to 48 percent women and 52 percent men. Not bad. But for those of us women who are older, the odds aren't as strong—on some sites the ratio can even be two men to every woman.[1]

Graciously, this isn't Vegas! Because you and I are loved deeply, beyond measure, no "odds" determine either our destiny or our satisfaction with the lives we're living now. If God has someone for you who you'll meet online, stats won't stop you from meeting him.

As a delicious confirmation of that fact, I want to share just a few words from the fabulous man that Vaneetha met on eHarmony and married. Joel raves:

> Before Vaneetha had told me about post-polio, I googled her and found her blog online. The post I read began, "I couldn't carry my plate to the table today. Some days I can do this. Some days I can't."
>
> When I read those words, I mused, "Okay. It's a fact. It doesn't change things."
>
> Vaneetha was the most interesting, incredible person I'd ever met. *Who cares if she can't carry her plate to the table. I can do that.* I was captivated by her depth of character. She was bright, articulate, and had a brilliant sense of humor. When we began chatting on the phone, our conversations, which could last for hours, were deeply meaningful ones. Maybe, I reasoned, it's because she's been through so much. I could see that she hadn't fallen apart during the most difficult seasons of her journey, and I valued that.

On the day Vaneetha and I were married, my joy was indescribable as I saw her walking toward me down the aisle, swaying side to side with her signature limp. On our wedding day we didn't know how long we would have while Vaneetha could still walk. We still don't know. So we've been purposeful about enjoying the kinds of experiences and travel that will become more difficult as her body declines, and I am thankful for each day we have together. Daily she continues to be God's good gift to me.

That's what I'm talking about.

NAVIGATING
ENDINGS

Sometimes good things fall apart so
better things can fall together.

—*Unknown*

twenty-five

ENDINGS

The Four Ways Every Online
Relationship Will Conclude

You are equipped with the resources you
need to navigate endings you choose
and those you don't choose.

On the day I was going on my first eHarmony date, I was picking up
a donation at the home of a friend who'd met her husband online.

"Daniele!" I called out with a glimmer in my eye. "I've got a
date tonight!"

I was expecting her to pat me on the back or give me a high five.

Instead, she rolled her eyes and said, "Get ready for three
hundred bad dates!"

My heart fell.

"Oh, no," I insisted, quickly calculating the hassle and general social discomfort that was guaranteed to come with three hundred dates. "That is not my plan at all. That sounds *horrible*."

I knew Daniele had had quite a colorful dating experience before meeting her husband. One guy she met showed up at the date predrunk and ordered water at the restaurant, bragging about how the clever scheme saved him money. While it was great that Daniele had landed a husband she loved on date 301, she'd put in an awful lot of cups of coffee, painfully awkward small talk, and chain restaurant food before landing him.

That's the lore-on-the-street math, people: *three hundred bad dates*.

My apologies for bringing math into something that's already as burdensome as online dating. It has to be done.

If you're looking for "the one," and you meet said "one" on your very first date, then congratulations to you! Those are some good odds right there. The rest of us are wild with envy that you don't have to go on the other 299 dates. But, statistically, that fairy tale isn't going to happen to most of us. For the majority of us, like Daniele, there will be a number of relationships that, necessarily, *end*. Whenever one person decides that the other is not for them, there is going to be an *ending*.

Supposedly it takes men just fifteen minutes to decide whether the first date is a bad one, it takes women nearly an hour to decide. Whether you figure it out before the waitress arrives at your table on that first-and-only date, or whether you discern it after you've been seeing a man for five months, the odds are good that someone in the equation will end the relationship.

Because . . . *three-hundred*.

So let's break down the way these relationships end. By my count, whenever you meet someone new, it can go one of four ways: you're both feeling it, you're both not feeling it, you're not feeling it, or he's not feeling it.

YOU'RE FEELIN' IT AND HE'S FEELIN' IT

The best-case scenario is that you both enjoy each other and want to continue the relationship until death do you part. You, my friend, are living the dream.

♀♂	You're feelin' it	You're not feelin' it
He's feelin' it	👍👍	
He's not feelin' it		

The other three possibilities, which do not last until the grave, are more imminent *endings*: neither of you want to move forward; he doesn't want to move forward; you don't want to move forward.

YOU'RE NOT FEELIN' IT AND HE'S NOT FEELIN' IT

In my opinion, the best one of these lesser three ends is when both of you are *not* feeling it.

♀♂	You're feelin' it	You're not feelin' it
He's feelin' it		
He's not feelin' it		♂👎 ♀👎

Hear me out.

Let's say you're driving home from the date, and you've decided that this isn't the guy for you. Part of you fears that because you were so witty and charming, Mr. NotTheOne is quickly going to be begging for a second date. Later, as you turn out the lights for bed, glancing at your phone one last time, you're relieved he hasn't followed up to gush about your sparkling wit and gentle spirit. The next day comes and goes, and you haven't heard back from Mr. NotTheOne.

That's when you realize that you've stumbled upon the very best non–fairy-tale scenario ending there is: *the two-way rejection*. It's my favorite lazy ending! No one's hopes are dashed and no one has to put on their grown-up panties and say the hard ending words. In my book, the double rejection is a very close second place to "till death do us part."

Of the four possible scenarios, the most *difficult* two are when one of you is feeling it and one is not. Ouch.

YOU'RE NOT FEELIN' IT AND HE'S FEELIN' IT

Over the last year and a half, there have been a few gentleman friends I've needed to release when they were feelin' it and I was not.

	You're feelin' it	You're not feelin' it
He's feelin' it		
He's not feelin' it		

Sometimes my sense that we weren't right for each other was so evident that I was eager to initiate the conversation to say our relationship wouldn't be moving forward. I never loved it, but I did what had to be done.

But other times when I knew someone wasn't right for me, I was more reluctant to let go. These men I'm thinking of, I actually liked very much. And they kind of dug me too. But in each case, I had a clear sense—because of God's leading, or because of my instincts, or because of cold hard evidence—that I needed to end the relationship.

Did the author of confusion hiss things like, "Maybe you'll never find anyone. Maybe you'll be alone forever. Maybe you should just settle for this one"? Yes. But I had to weigh those reservations against what I knew to be true in my deep places. I had to trust my gut. And my spirit. The act of letting go of someone who wasn't the right person for me was an act of trust in God. By humbly saying "not my will but yours be done" as I released someone, I was exercising trust in a God who knows me and loves me.

Trusting God while ending a relationship meant that I believed God would provide for me. Trusting God while ending a relationship meant that I believed God would provide for the other person. Trusting God while ending a relationship meant that if I was making a stupid mistake, God could redeem whatever mess I made. Endings require just as much trust as beginnings.

Every time I had to have one of these conversations, did I have kindness and compassion in my heart alongside all the anxiety, even if I bungled it up? Yes, I absolutely did. Did I always accomplish my mission with sophistication and grace? At least one male eyewitness is eager to testify that I did not. I did the best I could.

YOU'RE FEELIN' IT AND HE'S NOT FEELIN' IT

The fourth way relationships end is when we dig someone and he does not reciprocate the affection we have for him.

♀♂	You're feelin' it	You're not feelin' it
He's feelin' it		
He's not feelin' it	👎♂ 👍♀	

One day a charming man and I were chatting online. Because I am really proud of some of my clever banter, and because we were both a little quirky-clever, I was a bit surprised when ChapelHillCharlie said, "Nice chatting with you, but I don't think we're a match." The moment I read the words I felt that rush of hot *shame* blush across my face. It stung. I didn't like it. But then I moved on.

That was a teeny-tiny baby breakup. Others are worse. Whether it's eighteen years into a marriage or eighteen minutes into a conversation, being "let go" stinks.

Is it disappointing? Yes.

Does it hurt a little, and sometimes a lot? Yes.

But you know what? You can weather the end of a relationship with God's help. I hate that I have so much life experience in this area, both in and out of dating, but you can trust me. Not to brag, but I'm sort of an expert at being left. That's how I know that you can feel your feelings of sadness, anger, disappointment, loneliness, and fear. You can name and grieve what you've lost. You can heal, grow, and move forward.

I haven't been on three hundred dates yet. I beg God, daily, to spare me from that dreadful fate. There will be new beginnings for me—and more endings as well—that I'm confident I can weather. Whether I am the ender or the endee, I have the resources and resiliency to move forward with God's help. You do too.

Even when some wily phantom decides to ghost us.

twenty-six

"I'LL CHECK MY CALENDAR"

Signs a Guy Might Ghost

Though you can't reliably predict when a man
will ghost, several signs might be indicators.

Typically there is no way to predict when a man will ghost,
mysteriously disappearing as if into thin air. Though sometimes there will be clues. After living through it a few times,
I've paused to examine the evidence and have noticed a few
themes—but only in hindsight, never once, unfortunately, with
foresight. So while I've not been clever enough yet to see it coming, I'm gaining more tools to recognize it that I want to share
with you too.

HE STOPS *INITIATING* COMMUNICATIONS.

For several days before Smartie Sam ghosted, he'd gradually stopped initiating conversations with me each day. Because we'd really hit it off, I did *not* read the signs.

If a new friend has been eager to initiate a conversation or check in with you regularly, notice if that begins to change. I know that it's easy to rationalize, "He's probably busy at work"—especially when he says, verbatim, "I'm busy at work"—but if he's interested in pursuing a relationship, he'll find the time. So keep your eyes open when a man stops initiating conversations with you.

Note: Remember how there are a host of reasons a guy might be unresponsive? If he never responds to a first message, it's not too hard to let it go. If you've been chatting for days, it can feel more personal. Realistically, you might not ever know if his ghosting behavior is driven by malice, cowardice, thoughtlessness, or if he was suddenly kidnapped for a pricy ransom. The meaning you assign to his behavior, though, will affect the feelings you have about it.

THE NATURE OF HIS COMMUNICATIONS CHANGES.

Before Friendly Frank disappeared, he'd stopped sending those cute bitmojis of himself laughing hysterically in response to my witty comments. (Really, I should have caught that one. Because I'm hilarious.)

If a man's communications become less frequent, less lengthy, less personal, or less creative, that's worth noticing. There could be all kinds of reasons for a change—family matters, work responsibilities, commitments with children—but a change in the way a man communicates with you might also signal that he's not as invested in the relationship as you might wish to believe he is.

HIS ACTIONS COMMUNICATE SOMETHING DIFFERENT FROM HIS WORDS.

After months of chatting with Dave, I suggested we catch a local minor league baseball game. Dave said it sounded good and that he'd check his calendar. He never circled back about a game.

When the Professor came along, I didn't want a repeat of that messaging-for-months business without ever meeting up. So after chatting a bit, I suggested that we meet for a meal. When the Professor said he'd "check his calendar," I had a little bit of a PTSD reaction. Calendar-checking had not worked out so well for me. After all, I reasoned, to settle myself down, the Professor was probably very different from that flaky Dave. But after the calendar-checking suggestion, the Professor absolutely, 100 percent disappeared. Actions speak louder than words: pay more attention to what a man *does* than what he says.

HE PUTS OFF GETTING TOGETHER.

"I travel next week, but after that we can look at our calendars," looking4u assured me. *Yes*, I thought, *we can look at our calendars in two weeks.* But the way most calendars work, we could also just look at them *now*. (Fool me three times!) I made a note to myself on said electronic calendar to circle back with looking4u the following week. And when I did? Crickets. No word from the guy who had told me he was intrigued by my profile and would love the opportunity to get to know me.

In the end, if a guy ghosts, he ghosts. And in no world do you ever need to worry that, if you'd said or done something differently, he might have been the right guy for you. He wasn't. He really just wasn't. I know that for sure.

And if you've been ghosted, my hope is that it will inspire you to treat others better than you've been treated. Because at the end of *every* relationship, whether you are the ender or the endee, you can always choose to end it *well*. Keep reading to find out how.

I DID IT SO YOU DON'T HAVE TO

"I Listened to His Words Instead of Noticing His Actions"

On this dating journey I've heard the mantra "actions speak louder than words" referenced endlessly by women who've been hoodwinked by a man—who may or may not ever self-identify as a hoodwinker—after the man's actions, or inaction, trumped whatever he'd been saying with his words.

And although it's maddening, and sometimes heartbreaking, I don't think any of the guys I met were trying to be particularly deceptive. No, I choose to believe that, like me, they're doing the best they can. They're also just trying to find their way with whatever limited tools they have in their toolboxes.

But the best way to discern a man's true intentions—of which he may not yet be aware—is to notice what he *does*.

- Does he call you when he says he's going to call?
- Does he create that playlist for you that he offered to make?
- Does he follow through on arranging the plans he suggested? And, if he has to cancel, does he offer alternative arrangements?

If a man's words are different from his actions, download all the details with a girlfriend who can help you unpack it and discern whether or not you will choose to move forward.

twenty-seven

ENDING WELL

Be Grown, Be Clear, Be Kind

The best way to end relationships, either as the
ender or the endee, is to be grown, clear, and kind.

Strongman704 lived about twenty miles from me, in Raleigh,
North Carolina. We'd just connected online and were chatting
back and forth in real time as I made my lunch in the kitchen. We
were mostly unpacking the ins and outs of the flourishing courier
business he owned. We were about fifteen minutes into the chat
when I sent a message and instantly got a pop-up reply on my
phone that read: "You have been blocked by this user."

Wait, what?! I have been blocked?

Rage shot through my veins at the offense. I am *not* the girl
who gets blocked. He could just as easily have ghosted by going
silent and not replying to my final message rather than going to

the trouble of blocking me, on the app, like I was your everyday run-of-the-mill pervert.

My mind raced to fill in the blanks. I'd not asked Strongman704 for any kind of kinky special delivery that could have been misconstrued. The only possible reason I could conjure that I'd been blocked by Strongman704 was that our conversation was boring him. Honestly, the minutia of the local transport and delivery of time-sensitive legal documents bored me as well.

Although I don't have all the information about why I got blocked, the story I made up was that Strongman704 had tired of the conversation and instead of concluding it like a grown-up, he had chosen the easiest out. His behavior made me suspect I was dealing with a boy and not a man. Unfortunately, racking up a lot of calendar years does not make either a man *or* a woman.

Ending a conversation, a friendship, or a dating relationship requires maturity, good communication, and care. Whether the other person calls it quits or you politely decline that next date, I want to suggest that these endings can always be done *well*. Yes, getting dumped can hurt. And, yes, it also usually feels awkward and uncomfortable to let someone else know that you're not interested in moving forward. But what I want you to hear is that whether or not you're the person who ends the relationship, how you exit is up to you. In every relationship, you can choose to end well. Or, more accurately, you can do your very best to end well. You might blunder. He might receive your words in a spirit other than you intended. The best you can do is the best you can do.

Three rules govern a good goodbye: Be grown. Be clear. Be kind.

As you know, there are plenty of endings that don't end with maturity, clarity, or kindness.

Maybe it's that guy you dig who sends you a text every morning between 6:30 and 7:00. You know his birthday, and the names of his grandkids, and his most-hated NCAA basketball team. You've gone out a few times. You have a relationship you both seem to enjoy, then one day he simply stops responding to your texts. He ghosts.

Not grown.

Or maybe he breadcrumbs you. He's engaged for a bit, but then communication becomes sparse. But he'll be in touch occasionally, with no real interest in building a relationship. He offers words that suggest he likes you, but his actions suggest otherwise.

Not clear.

Or maybe he's that guy who makes plans and then he doesn't show. The earnest part of you wants to believe he's been hit and smashed by a city bus—a possibility that preserves both your dignity and his decency—but in your heart of hearts, you know he's not been killed by a bus. Which, honestly, feels a little bit disappointing.

Not kind.

A friend who weathered this journey a few years before me specified clear instructions in her dating profile for how to end a relationship. Brenda suggested to anyone reading, "When you're done, you're done. Have the courtesy to say so. You don't even have to give an explanation or excuse. Just be considerate and I'll do the same." Brenda told me, "I didn't fault anyone for telling me on the first date that they weren't interested in a second. I just smiled, said 'Thank you,' and moved on." Now that's what I'm talking about! Grown. Clear. Kind. When you're done with a relationship, say you're done. Whether you choose to end the relationship or that decision is made for you, I believe that you can weather the end of any relationship with grace.

So let's dish about the endings that go south. Specifically, how do you practice grace when someone else behaves badly?

If you've listened to country music, ever, you've probably heard at least one of these ballads about a relationship that goes south in the ugliest way. Like that gal in Carrie Underwood's song who really did a number on her ex's pretty little souped-up four-wheel drive. (But I do feel confident that, next time, he'll think before he cheats.) She suggests that he behaved badly first, so she replied in kind.

While you don't have any control over how someone else acts, you can always choose how you will react. Personally, I think the violent destruction of motor vehicles, though no doubt satisfying, is ill-advised. When someone treats you poorly, you choose whether you'll take the high road or the low road. For the purpose of this discussion, let's call destroying his automobile "the low road." Sure, it would feel great for a hot minute, but we can all agree it's kind of ugly. When we take the low road, we act immature. Or we're unclear. Or we're unkind.

Ghosting is low road.

Unmerited blocking is low road.

Saying you don't want to date, but that maybe you could still be friends and go to movies and ball games and things that seem an awful lot like dates, lacks clarity. (Sorry, SirGolf. I learned a lot of this the hard way.) Low road.

You get the idea.

Have I wanted to go full "low road"? Absolutely. With all my heart. When Frank ghosted after making plans to go out, I remembered that I knew what he did on Tuesday nights. On Tuesdays Frank went to open-mic night at Goodnights Comedy Club in Raleigh. And it just so happens that my secret superpower is stand-up comedy! So I fantasized about taking the stage one Tuesday night to perform my bit about how awful online dating is, then ripping off my wig and fake nose and mustache so that Frank would realize it was me! He'd try to get up and leave, but I'd call him out and ask him to stay seated and enjoy the show. I'd do my six-minute set and end with the funny, sad, maddening story of being ghosted, maybe even pointing him out in the audience to warn all the other single ladies, which is, I think, basically just community service, isn't it?

Admittedly, everything about my weird fantasy was textbook low road.

I'm ambivalent to report that, as of this writing, I haven't humiliated Frank at Goodnights. I wish I could say it was due to my stalwart character, or my unflagging trust in God's justice, but if I'm keeping it real, that's not it at all. It's really my pride that holds me back.

If I go into full cray-cray warrior mode—even if completely justified—I know that it allows the other person to say to himself, *Well, I really dodged a bullet with that one!* And really, that's it. It's the bullet-dodging. That's what keeps me from getting all ugly with men who've behaved unkindly. I refuse to give them the satisfaction of being able to tell themselves that *they're* bullet dodgers. Nope, not on my watch. When you choose the low road, you lose; when you choose the high road, you win.

I actually had to choose low road or high road this week when that guy who'd ghosted for six months circled back. (I won't go into the sordid details, but I do encourage you to make up some outrageous details in your mind.) He simply texted out of the blue, casually offering, "Hey stranger, how are you doing?" He acted as if he hadn't behaved like a real [insert ugly-language-of-your-choice here]. (Reader girl, I can see how you're doing a lot of the creative work in this paragraph, and I appreciate that.) And while choosing the high road might possibly have meant kindly reminding him that as a direct result of his actions, our relationship had come to an unceremonious close, this time I didn't. This time I chose not to respond and blocked his number. I just didn't want to expend the energy, and that was the highest road I could take.

Some endings stink. Sometimes you *will* feel lousy. Go ahead and have all those feels. But then remember that you are the only one who gets to decide how you respond. That's what you're in charge of. You can't control how other people treat you, but you can control how you respond.

IMPLEMENTING SIX HEALTHY PRACTICES

Love recognizes no barriers. It jumps hurdles, leaps fences, penetrates walls to arrive at its destination full of hope.

—*Maya Angelou*

twenty-eight

FRIENDSHIP

Rolling with Your Support Squad

A valuable practice for the journey is
enlisting the support of girlfriends.

On this dating journey, whenever I have an impulse—to ask a guy to coffee, or to turn down a second date, or to ignore someone because I'm miffed that they posted a dumb picture of their shoes—I'll run it past my friend Olivia. Invariably, she will instruct me to do the diametric opposite of whatever my natural impulse might have been.

One hundred percent of the time, she is right.

Olivia is one of the women on my support squad who attempts to help me not screw up the whole thing. I couldn't do this dating journey without my support squad of friends who are with me along the way. I'm delighted to report that it's not like a nonprofit board that has regular monthly meetings. In fact, a few of the most important women on my team don't even know one another! (As someone who hates to attend meetings, this is really my kind of committee.) The squad also includes a beautiful diversity of friends. Each member of my support squad brings different gifts.

If a man was convicted of a misdemeanor during college, Emily is going to sniff it out.

If a man who claims to be a widower really *isn't*, Cathy will discover it.

If a guy doesn't exist at all, because he's a sneaky guy trying to catfish me, Lizbeth will realize it before I do.

If a man doesn't think I'm the cat's meow, Lisa will assure me—based on nothing at all—that he's not worth worrying about.

And if I text Susan that a man has behaved inappropriately, she's going to text back all the naughty words she'd like to say to him. Which I secretly love.

Not for one moment do I take these amazing steadfast women for granted. And that is because I haven't always had them. Well, I've *had* female friends, but because of my own insecurities I didn't always trust their love for me. I first noticed it when I was about twenty. Four or five college girlfriends were hanging out in my dorm room late one evening, operating on too little sleep and too much caffeine, when the idea of taking an epic summer road trip together was born. But a little voice in my head suggested that I wouldn't *really* be welcome to join the adventure. It was the same little voice that said mean things like, "You're a burden," "They don't really want you," and "They care for each other more than they care for you." The seeds of those cruel echoes had nothing to do with my friends and everything to do with the early losses I'd suffered. That summer, though, in the back seat of a blue Chevy Nova driving up Pacific Coast Highway, somewhere between San Diego and Vancouver my friends' care began to soften my stubborn heart until even I could no longer deny their evident love for me. Graciously, through these angels and other friends, God would continue to nurse my fractured heart to health.

More than two decades after our road trip, my husband of eighteen years left me. During that particular season, though, I had been putting more energy into being a wife and a mom and a writer than I had into my female friendships. (It happens.) But of course I never needed female friendships more than I did in that moment. I have a clear memory of standing in my kitchen musing, *Even though I haven't been nurturing my friendships, I'm pretty sure that there are women who love me and will show up for me during this awful season.* That hunch has proved true in more ways than I can count, because the female friends God had given me in that season loved me fiercely in the wake of my marriage falling apart.

In the same way I'm seeing it today on the dating journey, each one offered a different kind of care I so desperately needed. One fierce friend got all angry and riled up about each injustice I suffered (obviously, this is Susan). Another friend gently offered the name of a divorce attorney who would protect me in ways I didn't even know I needed during my amicable divorce. One friend reflected for me the sadness I could no longer avoid. Another delivered flowers on that first Valentine's Day after my husband left and hasn't missed one yet. God orchestrated these beautifully unique ways of loving me through this diverse crew of women on whom I could rely.

Of course, I had to choose to *accept* all they offered. Had I gotten stuck in "they don't really care for you," I would have missed all the good God showered on me through these precious women. Receiving God's love through others requires that I *accept* God's love through others. Today, six years later, I can't imagine dating without these women.

A lot of times they name or confirm an intuitive hunch I may already be sensing but have failed to notice and heed. And the good instincts of these women are how I learned to begin to trust my own gut.

RULE OF THUMB: NOTICE WHAT YOU DON'T TELL YOUR GIRLS

Give special attention to anything you're not eager or willing to tell your girlfriends. If the only time a guy calls you is at midnight, and you don't want your girls to know that, that's worth noticing. If you're hiding the fact that you've picked up the check all three times you've been out with a man, that's a red flag. If you're not telling them that you're driving the forty-mile round trip to his apartment five times a week, pay attention. Often your support team is going to value you even more than you value yourself.

twenty-nine

INTUITION

Trusting Your Gut

A valuable practice for the journey is
paying attention to your instincts.

Whenever I am getting to know a man early on in a potential dating situation, and I'm just not feeling it, I want to have a rational
reason, for myself, about why I don't want to pursue the relationship. There are endless reasons, but here are a few.

- He's not striking me as being very interesting.
- He has a pattern of infidelity that doesn't seem to cause
  him concern.
- He has thrown back four liquor drinks over lunch.
- He said he'd call Sunday night and he didn't call.

Everyone has different thresholds for what qualifies as a deal-breaker, but very early on any of those could be reason enough for me to say, "Nice meeting you," and leave it at that. But I also recognize that the discernment process requires humility. It requires me to admit that I really can't know everything about who someone is.

Maybe he's the kind of guy who really shines on the second date.

Maybe I can't yet see what God has done in his life since the last time he committed adultery.

Maybe the heavy lunch drinking is an anomaly.

Maybe he didn't call Sunday because he was flying across the country to care for his sister after her emergency hip-replacement surgery. I don't really know.

Admittedly, some of these are statistically unlikely. But I want to make room for the chance that I am not seeing the whole picture of who someone is. (And because I was born with a defective "obvious common sense" chromosome, I've learned to notice and imitate the behaviors of some girlfriends on my squad who are savants at discerning what is obvious to someone with naturally good instincts.)

But I'm also learning to make room for another possibility. Sometimes there are legitimate reasons a relationship should not move forward that simply aren't objective, rational, or quantifiable. This means that at times my gut is telling me not to move forward even when I can't conveniently "tag" a situation with one of my justifiable objections. Which is both a little humbling and a bit disconcerting. Honestly, it's not a strategy with which I have a lot of experience. No parent or mentor or teacher ever coached me to trust my gut. I mean, what even is that, anyway?

When I pause to silence the wordy voices in my head and the hungry yearnings of my heart, I notice this other sensory organ—my gut—that's giving me information.

It's instinct.

It's discernment.

It's wisdom.

It's conscience.

It's intuition.

It may even be God's Spirit.

Trusting your gut is knowing, instinctually, whether a situation is wrong or right. Whether you're choosing a grad school, or a church home, or a therapist, or a potential romantic partner, pausing to notice what your insides are saying is one way to seek discernment. When you pay attention to your gut, God's Spirit can prompt you to move forward, to stay put, or to step back.

I've been noodling on this business about trusting my gut this week because I've spent way too many hours trying to come up with the words, the logic, to let Trevor know why I don't see our relationship moving forward. In my mind, I imagine he'll demand an explanation. Because on paper, we seem like we'd be really good together. We like each other. We could talk for hours. But there's also this knowing sense I have in my gut.

This one doesn't have my name on it.

This one's not for me.

Something's a bit off, though I'm struggling to name the reasons.

There's someone who's going to be a better match.

Right now I don't sense he's for me.

After some hits and misses, when I have bungled things up because I was unwilling to notice and honor what my gut was telling me, I've now given myself permission to be guided, in part, by my gut.

I've also given myself the generous gift of taking the occasional break from dating.

I DID IT SO YOU DON'T HAVE TO

"I Stayed in It Longer Than I Should Have"

I'll be the first to admit that I hung on to my friendship with Ernie for too long. I was a newbie to online dating, and I liked the attention. If my gut was telling me to step away from the relationship, I wasn't paying attention. In my mind, it was the *beginning* of something more substantial than the texting and occasional phone call. Except, in the end, it really wasn't. Beyond breeding intimacy too quickly, chronic texting gives the person on the other end—or, honestly, on *your* end—lots of time to think of a calculated or clever reply. It's just not the same as spending face-to-face time together. Make the time and space to get together. And if you can't, or if he can't, read the signs.

thirty

SABBATH

Practicing App Sabbath

A valuable practice for the journey is
pausing to take a break from the apps.

Streaked in blue-and-white war paint, the face of thirteenth-century Scotland's Sir William Wallace flashes with fury and determination. His wild, unkempt shoulder-length hair whips in the wind like a lion's mane. Baring every tooth in his mouth, clutching a metal sword, Wallace roars a fierce battle cry before leading hordes of brave young soldiers to slaughter or be slaughtered.

That guy with the makeup? That's me.

And online dating.

There are only two ways this thing will end: I will either be victorious or I will die trying.

But I know that not every soldier in the conflict bears the

fierce determination and irrational resolve that Wallace and I have. I'm talking about girlfriends who've admitted to me that they've needed to take a break from dating apps. And I don't mean for a minute. I don't mean "take-a-cool-refreshing-swig-from-the-canteen-and-charge-back-into-battle." I mean they scrap the apps for three months. Or for three years. Or delete them forever.

When I'd hear these reports, I'd tend to feel a little smug about my warrior ethic. About never stopping. Did William Wallace stop? Did Martin Luther King Jr. take a two-year break? Did Mahatma Gandhi step away for a luxury cruise vacation? (I realize I have situated myself in some very impressive company. I felt it was necessary.)

No, they didn't stop.

And neither would I.

I reasoned that the only way to get off the apps for good was to stay on the apps until I found the good.

That's how my warrior logic went.

But once I was about eighteen months in, I was tired. Bruised. Bleeding a little. Disappointed. Hopeless. So yeah, I took a break. I cried uncle. *Sir William Wallace, you're better than I.*

A weeklong series of unfortunate events led up to my first dating app sabbath.

Tuesday night I had a great conversation on the phone with a pretty cool guy. I loved his voice and I really liked who he seemed to be. But because his heart was still healing from a seismic loss, he confessed that he wasn't yet ready to be in a relationship. As we hung up, he remarked that he was glad to have made a new friend. I knew, of course, that the word *friend* was the kiss of romantic death.

Wednesday I was scheduled to do dinner with someone I'd gone out with six months earlier. I knew he was a busy guy, so I assumed he'd check in on Wednesday to shore up the details. But no details were ever shored. I didn't hear back from him and we didn't go out. To complicate matters a bit *emotionally*, our date was to have landed on February 13, the sacred eve of Valentine's Day. Hear me: in no fantasy world did I think he was my valentine. And despite my rage-against-the-machine resistance to the commercialized manipulation that goes along with Valentine's Day, part of my heart still *felt* the sting.

Thursday, I woke up sad and mad. I was sad because of the recent disappointments. I was mad that I felt sad on dumb old Valentine's Day. It's very complicated to be a liberated woman. But I soldiered on. And that night Olivia and I went to a rooftop club in downtown Durham where we enjoyed some live jazz and delicious appetizers and sipped on yummy drinks. Like the victors we are, we both agreed that we were winning at Valentine's Day.

Then . . . Friday. (Don't worry, the week is almost over.)

I'd gone to a girls' basketball game at Riverside High School to cheer on a young friend when I noticed the weekend "loneliness" starting to creep over me. I scanned the bleachers for any eligible single dads—with no plan whatsoever for what I'd do if I actually found one. And like any creepy sports mom worth her salt, I checked out the refs for wedding rings. But I walked out of the gymnasium the same way I'd walked in: single. Any other week I might have bounced out of Riverside, zipped through the McDonald's drive-thru for an ice cream cone, and happily gone home to paint a masterpiece or write a book. But, on February 15, I was feeling sad.

Once I reached the privacy of my automobile, the deep anguish that had been living behind my eyes began to swell, pressing and demanding release. I didn't see it coming, but as I drove down Guess Road my grief erupted into full-blown mascara-drippy sobs. And rather than fill the void with ice cream, I allowed it.

I felt the pain of being bruised and battered by the dating journey.

I felt lonely, wanting so badly to share life with someone.

I felt a deep longing for someone who was going to stick around.

I felt a yearning for someone who would love me.

I felt grief that I hadn't been desired, in my marriage, the way a woman wants to be desired.

In case it's not clear, I really got a lot of mileage out of that particular eruption of sadness.

Though the volcanic weeping didn't last more than ten or fifteen minutes, the deep loneliness settled in for a weekend visit, staying through Saturday and Sunday. Although I felt sad, I was still able to function. I wrote words. I attended a board meeting. I worshiped God. I made cards and posters for neighbors. I ate too much Italian food at Maggiano's for my daughter's twentieth birthday celebration. But for those few days, I dwelt in the shadow of loneliness.

So when I woke up on Monday, I had the sense God was inviting me to take a break from dating apps. God was welcoming me to set down my sword. And wipe off my war paint. To step away from the battlefield, maybe take a shower and condition my hair, with the trust that the outcome of the endeavor did not depend on me. While that may seem pretty obvious to you, it felt wildly counterintuitive to me.

It also felt *right*.

Stepping back, I accepted what was clearly God's gracious invitation to practice sabbath by taking a break from the apps. It was a way for me to not just pay lip service to trusting God for my present and my future, but to *actively* trust God. I see that, to the eye of a stranger, it looked more like laziness than action. That's what's so freakin' counterintuitive about it. Taking a break from the dating apps is an opportunity to actively trust God. As tightly as I clutch my smartphone, scrolling and winking and clicking and liking, a break reminds me that God's plan for me does not depend on the apps.

It was a great week. I rested. I healed. I noticed God's presence with me. And I was freed up to just *be*, without all the *doing*. I highly recommend it. Three months later, a month before my fiftieth birthday, God called me to a monthlong sabbath.

When I started using online dating apps, the age on each one of my profiles was forty-eight. I knew I did not want to still be on the apps when that number rolled over into the next decade—both because I'm impatient and also because I liked being the hot young babe on the sites for old people. But when fifty was actually approaching, I realized that what was even more important to me than "finding someone while I was still in my forties," was to not be scrambling frantically to find someone while I was still in my forties. Make sense? I wanted the turn of the decade to be about giving gratitude to God for the beautiful life I've been allowed to live, and not about whether or not I'd found my boo. With great delight, thirty days before my half-a-century birthday, I gladly either quit completely or hid my profile on every app. Then, for the month leading up to my big day, I ignored the apps. It was awesome.

I've also accepted other kinds of invitations from the Spirit to take a break from the apps. Each time I am reminded that I don't put my trust in a carefully worded profile or whatever goofy selfie I've taken where I've successfully disguised any hint of a double chin. Taking a break from my grippy control of the whole situation, by pausing from the apps, is one way I am choosing to trust God.

The other *active* part of each app sabbath was to pay attention to God. That's always sort of a work in progress with me. But I made a twofold commitment to God during these breaks: I will listen; I will trust. That's it. That's my part. I promised to listen for God's voice when I prayed, through Scripture, through friends, as I wrote, and in any other way he might want to speak. I also let God know that I was willing to trust in God's goodness.

While God might invite you to practice sabbath in any number of creative ways, here are five that have worked well for me at different moments on my journey.

1. DAILY SABBATH: USE APPS AFTER 6 P.M.

When I noticed that a lot of my days were beginning by checking my phone to see if I'd gotten any attention while I'd been sleeping, it became clear I needed to do something differently. When I chose to turn off notifications and wait until after 6 p.m. to peek each day, I experienced real freedom.

2. WEEKLY SABBATH: NO APPS ON SUNDAYS.

Ever peek at a dating app while sitting in a church pew Sunday morning? Red flag, friend, red flag. Once I tried taking a break on Sundays, I was hooked. After that I regularly welcomed the gift of breaking from the work of attending to the apps on Sundays, the same way I take a break from the regular work of the week.

3. FIVE-DAY SABBATH: USE APPS ONLY ON FRIDAYS AND SATURDAYS.

Another way I experienced freedom was by avoiding the apps Sunday through Thursday. It allowed me to stay focused on God, and work, and the real relationships in my life and still explore new friendships on Fridays and Saturdays.

4. WEEKLONG SABBATH: BREAK FROM APPS FOR A WEEK.

That first weeklong break from the apps disrupted my addiction to them and gave my heart a welcome breather.

5. ONE-MONTH SABBATH: NO APP USE FOR A MONTH.

Using no apps for a month gave me time to recalibrate and refocus.

Taking a break from dating apps allows us to be present to the present.

I don't know how God will lead you, but I'm confident that God longs to be gracious to you. And taking a beautiful sabbath rest from the work of the apps might free up some space for you to receive God's graciousness.

In the meantime, before we ever meet the man of our dreams, we are being given opportunities to *love well*.

thirty-one

LOVE

Being for *Others*

A valuable practice for the journey is
to love God and love others.

My single friend Sandra was shopping for a car one Saturday
afternoon, and Alex the Salesman was particularly friendly and
chatty. He took an interest in her parents being from Nigeria and
also in her being a Christian. While his interest might normally
have been flattering, Alex the Salesman was wearing a wedding
ring. Not cool. (Stick with me, because this story is about to get
a lot better.) Before Sandra left the dealership, Alex the Salesman
said, "Can I introduce you to someone?" When Sandra hesitantly
agreed, Alex dipped into the office and came out with a friend,
another salesman, whose parents were also from Nigeria. The two
chatted for a while and really hit it off. Best feature? No wedding

ring! Alex the Salesman did what we want all of our friends to do for us, right? We want them to be *for* us. And that can mean introducing us to someone awesome. And that's what Alex did.

One of the pitfalls I've stumbled into during this dating season is to become self-focused. I've spent more time than I'd prefer to admit choosing the best selfies, scrolling through apps, and basically thinking about *me* and what I want. Which is exhausting. To a degree it's necessary, but that's not who I want to be. I want to be a person who's *for* others, when I'm not dating and when I am dating, when I'm single and when I'm coupled. And the beautiful double-win of purposing to love others well on this journey is that it blesses them and, because it helps me get my eyes off myself, it also blesses me.

After hearing what Alex the Salesman did for my friend Sandra—or really did for *his* friend, since Sandra is such a prize—I've taken a stab at connecting single women friends with guys I believe to be good matches. (No wedding bells yet, but I definitely fantasize about that eventual wedding where the bride and groom thank me profusely for changing their lives forever. I lower my eyes in humility, but inside I'm proud as a matchmaking peacock.) I can be *for* other women by praying for them and taking a genuine interest in them. I can be *for* other women by encouraging them during dry desert seasons. I can be *for* them as I celebrate their wins and grieve their losses, just like they do for me. When I am for other women, my eyes aren't on myself.

The same way I want to be for other women, I also want to be *for* the men I'm meeting. Even if I sense that a man is not the one who's meant for me, my prime directive, and yours, is still *love*. In one case, that meant helping someone in a career similar to mine take the next step forward on his professional journey. For another, it meant helping a man get one step closer to finding the woman who *was* the right one for him. About six months after SirGolf and I had gone out, I saw his profile pop up on a different site. But when I read it again, I realized that it failed to include some of the things I'd discovered about him on our date that really made him special. It didn't mention the cool friendships he'd kept up over three decades. It didn't say that he'd recently taught his granddaughter how to drive. It didn't reference his big dreams for developing a really unique business. So, naturally, I messaged him to ask him if I could offer a new and improved "About Me" profile narrative. He agreed, and I think we put together a really strong profile. SirGolf, I got you. When I am for the men I'm meeting, my eyes aren't on myself.

Because of who my friend Lonnie is, it is natural for her to invest in the men she is meeting. After one man shared some of the ways he was still stuck in the bitterness of his divorce, Lonnie had the opportunity to share with him about the journey of forgiveness she'd experienced with her dad that had transformed her life. She knew firsthand that, without forgiveness, bitterness can eat us alive, and she cared for her date by giving him a glimpse of another possibility. Lonnie models for me what it looks like to be generous in caring for someone else we meet while dating.

A week when I was feeling particularly lonely and disheartened about dating, I was invited to an evening dessert gathering to learn more about a new ministry, among people with and without disabilities, that a few friends were being called to launch. As David and Kelli and Ryan shared about what they sensed God was up to, I felt my insides come alive. As the team spoke about their needs, the Spirit quickened my heart about some of the ways

I could support them. After the meeting, I texted Kelli, "I'm so tired of thinking about myself. Nothing could have been better than tonight." That little opportunity to lift my eyes off myself, by joining the kingdom-building that God was doing in our community, was a beautiful gift I received from God's gracious hands.

Let's be *for* the men we meet. Let's be generous to other women. Let's keep our eyes open for how we're called to participate in the story that's bigger than our own. The best antidote for the temptation to be all about ourselves is to be generous toward others. So until we cross paths with Mr. Right, let's practice loving well. And as we do, let's purpose to be who we really are.

thirty-two

AUTHENTICITY

When You're Spicy and When You're Mild, Be Who You Really Are

Despite voices that lie, you are neither
"too much" nor "not enough."

"I've never had much of a filter and I have a strong sense of justice," Becky explained when we met.

So obviously, I liked her right away: #nofilter and #justice.

She added, "It was part of what brought Keith and me together, but I wasn't sure that any other guy would actually want that—especially if it came with two kids."

Becky's husband had died when they were pregnant with their second child, and I was curious what her experience of dating had been like since then.

Becky offered, "I've lost count of the men who want to 'start fresh' with someone without kids. Most times I could barely hold my tongue, wanting to lecture them that everyone in their twenties and thirties has baggage."

Compared to the massive oversize freight some people my age are lugging around, I *wish* I was carrying the airy featherweight totes some of those young whippersnappers are sporting. Not *Becky's* bag, but other people's little duffels.

Becky added, "It seems that, in general, men see a widow with kids and assume that I'm only in it for their financial stability."

Her experience, she assured me, resonated with that of many of her younger widowed friends.

Since there are very few guys *my age* who want to procreate by "starting fresh"—though there are a *few* with their heart set on making babies—I hadn't before encountered a man resistant to dating a widow with kids.

My friend Grace, about a decade older than Becky, is also a widow. A soccer mom like me, she also sits on the back row of the Bulldogs' little stack of bleachers, which you might recall is the birthplace of my readiness to date. As we chatted about dating, Grace proudly announced, "I bring a hell of a lot less baggage than people think." (I hadn't been the one to bring up luggage. It was all her.) She and her widow friends dish about guys, and she explained, "We notice that men have run screaming from the widow, thinking we were moneybags."

Thinking I'd misunderstood, I clarified, "Moneybags?"

She explained, "They think we're loaded."

These widows can't catch a break. Am I right?

Unfounded financial assumptions aside, both women identified one of the lies that many women who are dating also hear: "You're *too much*."

If we're not widowed, we might fear that our fiery opinions are too much for a man to handle. (Even if we're obviously right.) Or we worry our gaggle of children—or the one child who feels like a gaggle—makes us undateable. Or we fear that our unique medical needs make us less attractive. We fear that we are too much, and a voice named "you're-too-much" confirms our suspicion.

But what's particularly wily is that there's another gal badgering us who is *friends* with "you're-too-much." And her name is, "you're-not-enough."

When we're lying awake in bed at night, she whispers that whatever we wrote in our dating profile isn't enough.

Or she intimates that in that first awkward phone conversation we won't be *witty* enough.

Or she suggests that when he sees us in person he'll decide that our bodies aren't fit enough.

Like her catty friend "you're-too-much," she's a real bully. Am I right?

The whole double-edged lie of enoughness—that we are simultaneously "too much" and "not enough"—is sticky and twisty and tangly. And more than a little evil.

And while these deceptive gals are nothing if not persistent, we actually don't have to be bossed around by them. When we notice those voices, we can replace them with what is more true: "I am, and I am becoming, exactly who God made me to be."

Beloved, you are *not* too much. I know this because, despite whatever you are carrying, you are, in every moment, altogether worth loving. And you are also not *not enough*. I know this for the same reason. Despite whatever you fear you are lacking, there's nothing that can make you unlovable. Because these twin bullies are so bossy, you might have to put them in their place a few times. But I promise you, truth is on your side.

As she thought about her future, Becky offered, "My friends and counselor have been gracious in helping me learn to see that my resilience and my hilarious and precocious children will only be assets to someone someday." Now that's what I'm talking about! A perfect example of choosing what is *most true*.

Though it can be tempting to disguise or minimize or inflate or mute who you really are, don't do it, precious one.

Be.

Who.

You.

Really.

Are.

thirty-three

HOPE

Not Quitting Before the Miracle

A valuable practice for the journey is
living with hope—because we trust a
God who does unlikely things.

At the beautiful age of sixty-five, writer Anne Lamott got married for the first time after meeting the man of her dreams on a dating site for adults over fifty.

So that lovely miracle happened.

Anne Lamott was wed to her beloved in a lush redwood grove, surrounded by family and friends. Her matted dirty-blonde locks were pulled back out of her face, and she wore a beautiful, flowing, lacy ivory dress she'd bought on eBay. So she pretty much got the fairy-tale ending for which gals like us hope.

After.

Waiting.

Sixty-five.

Years.

Because I've been married, I do know that marriage is not all butterflies and roses. Whether or not you've been married, you know this too. I'm sure that either Anne or her groom will still drop their sweaty socks on the bathroom floor and leave dirty dishes in the kitchen sink. Still, her wonderful wedding is a hundred times better than the boring old Disney fairy-tale ones because the bride is old, her physique is flawed, parts are sagging, and her skin is weathered. (Sorry, Anne. Facts.)

Some old gals like us who hear Anne's story might grumble that another good man is off the market. Others will dismiss it as a rare miracle that's statistically very unlikely. And some of us will celebrate the goodness, and hope, and possibility of a story that's something like our own. For what it's worth, I think it's worth celebrating. Stories like Anne's can fuel the flicker of hope in our hearts as we see what's possible for those who believe—not just for those who believe in romantic fairy-tale magic, but for those who believe in what God can do. Our hope is kindled when we see the grace of God in action.

It's how we're wired. Our theological imaginations are *meant* to be ignited when we see God at work. We see it when a woman named Sarah conceives a son at the age of ninety. We're reminded again of what's possible when Elizabeth, whom one extrabiblical source puts at eighty-eight years of age, conceives the little embryo who will become John the Baptist. And we also recognize holy possibility when a spicy, irreverent sixty-five-year-old woman with a brood of cats and runaway anxieties finds love.

Each one is a story of God's unlikely faithfulness to a woman who trusted God. In case I need to spell it out, the *other* ladies—Cinderella, Snow White, and Princess Aurora—are *fictional*. But Sarah and Elizabeth and Anne are real women who trusted God. And just as the biblical stories we find in Scripture testify to the goodness of a God of surprises, Anne's story of God's unlikely grace also belongs to the people of God.

I see a poignant lesson in here for those of us who are still waiting. And I guess you might not catch it if you're not familiar with Anne Lamott. So what's important for you to know is that she didn't waste a lot of time *not* living her life. I mean, sure, she dodged having to attend stupid parties, like any self-respecting introvert, but she *lived* her life. She spoke her truth. She loved her friends. She used her gifts. She raised a son. And, along the way, she even raised a little hell. She lived, and is living, the fruitful, one-of-a-kind life that she was made to live.

Those of us who are still waiting, hoping to find the love of our lives, can take our cues from Anne. Moment by moment, we are being called to live well *before* the fairy-tale ending. As a woman who, for decades, *did* want to be married, Anne discovered how to balance the "right now" and the "not yet." She figured out how to *live* the life she'd been given even as she hoped for something else. When asked what advice she would give to gals like us, Anne Lamott said, "If you're paying attention and making your own life as beautiful and rich and fun as it can be, you might just attract someone who's doing the same thing."[1] Isn't that delicious? That's exactly what we're called to do daily, living what Jesus calls "life that really is life"—even as we keep our eyes open for what might be next. Daily balance living your rich, beautiful life that is *now*, even as you hope for what might be *next*.

On Twitter, the day before her wedding, Anne Lamott

exhorted, "Never ever give up, no matter how things look or how long they take. Don't quit before the miracle."[2]

Anne didn't quit.

Sarah didn't quit.

Elizabeth didn't quit.

I didn't quit.

Don't quit, you.

You got this.

RESOURCES FOR THE JOURNEY

Eight Prayers for the Dating Journey

As your dating journey develops, so will your own conversations with God. When I feel sad, or psyched, or disappointed, or anxious, it really helps to be able to release it all to the One who cares. Here are a few starter prayers that might help you pray.

NOT MY WILL BUT YOURS

"Yet not my will, but yours be done" (Luke 22:42b).

If ever a passage from Holy Scripture has been taken out of context and twisted for utility's sake, this is the one. We humbly appropriate it when we want a promotion at work. We borrow it when we want our lowball offer on a new house to be accepted. And we prayerfully twist it in the hopes of meeting the man of our dreams.

After Jesus shared a final meal with his disciples, he went to the Mount of Olives to pray. He knew what was to come, and he begged, "Father, if you are willing, take this cup from me" (Luke 22:42a). He knew he was about to face the brutal violence of the cross, so he asked his Father to spare him. That's the legit biblical context for this story, girlfriends.

After his heart-wrenching request, Jesus resolved to follow God and said, "Yet not my will, but yours be done" (Luke 22:42b). While I'm not willing to *publicly* name any parallels between Jesus' words about his upcoming crucifixion and my experiences with online dating, I do want to imitate Jesus' spiritual presence before his Father. His posture toward God—on his knees, hands held open, eyes to heaven—is how I, and we, can imitate Jesus when we pray.

Acknowledging the blatant appropriation, I encourage you to assume Jesus' openhearted posture when you pray: on your knees, hands held open, eyes to heaven. (If your knees give you trouble, open hands and tilted eyes will suffice.)

I'M LONELY

My amazing friend Ella, the one I shared about who was so transparent about her loneliness (chapter 23), has blessed me so much with her thoughts on singleness. (Gosh, I love it when others keep it real and don't try to spiritualize what just really sucks.) She offered, "When I feel and notice my loneliness and desire for a lover, a companion, I talk aloud to God. I tell him how I feel, shed a few tears, and ask him to come alongside me to fill those empty spaces." Because she uses a wheelchair, Ella also verbalizes to God that it would take a very special man to fill that space, and then politely requests that, if he is out there, God would kindly orchestrate the introduction. She continued, "I then thank him for life, joy, laughter, and all the opportunities and experiences I'm given to show his love to others every day."

I think Ella's response is the most beautiful model of a "lonely" prayer I could imagine. She shares the loneliness with God, asks God to meet the deep needs of her heart, welcomes God to provide a friend to love her, and expresses gratitude for all that God has given to her. I'm not going to say that Ella is a Christian prayer wizard, but if you thought the same thing, then who would I be to argue? God welcomes prayers where we honestly confess our loneliness, offering it to him.

SEND SOMEONE OR TAKE THIS DESIRE FROM ME

After becoming single again, my friend Cherrie was given a prayer by another woman that she prayed on the regular: Either send someone or take this desire from me.

You read that right. Cherrie boldly pointed her finger to heaven and gave God two options for how to handle the situation. Kinda bossy, don't you think?

I won't lie: I *really* like Cherrie's prayer. Although it does sound sassy, it ultimately acknowledges that God is the one-and-only authority over our lives on earth. Whether God gives her a man to marry or removes the desire from her, both feel . . . right. Both options allow God's lovingkindness to shine upon Cherrie. To shine upon me. Shine upon you.

In her book *Teach Us to Want*, Jen Pollock Michel claims that when God groans for the faithfulness of his people—"Oh, that their hearts would be inclined to fear me and keep all my commands always!" (Deut. 5:29)—God is longing for the transformation of their hearts' *desires*.[1] That—transforming the desire of my heart—is something that God has done for me in the past, and something I'm also asking God to do in this season . . . even if I happen to think Cherrie's prayer is kind of bossy.

HELP ME TO SEE WHAT YOU SEE

We all need help "seeing" God's desires for our lives clearly.

I, for one, can get very enamored with a gentleman's appearance. Sometimes that can make me less discerning about his other qualities. I wish this weren't the case, but on more than one occasion it has proven to be true.

I have to remember that the flip side is also true: a man might not be Hollywood handsome—he may not be *movie-star* attractive—but he may possess all of the qualities that actually sustain a long-term loving relationship. When I think of women I've known who've met someone fantastic in their fifties, the most solid, fruitful, enduring relationships are those built with a man who was specifically *not* movie-star attractive. (Which, if you didn't figure it out, includes virtually *everyone*.)

We need help seeing clearly because it's possible our "poor vision" may not be only about physical attractiveness. It may be that when we're scrolling through potential matches online, we only "look" at men who have graduate degrees. Or we only "see" men who match our own ethnicity. Or we only "notice" those whose job titles are the kind that net six figures.

We need help seeing clearly.

When your finger opens a dating app, consider praying, *Help me to see what you see.*

TAKE MY EYES OFF MYSELF

There's something about the process of putting ourselves in the dating space, seeking the attention of others, that tempts us to become a little too preoccupied with ourselves. Truly, if anyone would have told me two years ago that I would have taken as many trying-too-hard selfies as I have, I wouldn't have believed them. And it's not just the photos; I'm spending actual time, money, and energy purchasing something called "blush," and painting my nails, and plucking rogue body hairs. When I notice that I'm becoming overly consumed with *me*, I pray, asking God's help to free me from self-absorption. When we become preoccupied with ourselves, we can ask God, *Take my eyes off myself.*

GUIDE MY NEXT STEP

The big idea of Emily P. Freeman's book *The Next Right Thing* is that even when we struggle to find clarity in some of the big decisions we face, we can always choose to do the *next right thing.* So . . . the dating example of a seismic, life-changing decision is, "Should I say 'yes' to his marriage proposal?" Ideally, though, as we've been getting to know someone, we've asked God's direction in the smaller decisions we've been making: *Does he seem to be a person of character? Has he invested in friendships? Is he generous and kind?* While it's maybe super-obvious to you, I want to encourage you to seek God's direction on the smaller decisions you're making each day. Invite God to lead you as you purpose to choose the next right thing.

WHY, OH LORD?

While the title of this prayer may have led you to believe that it is the ever-popular "Why, Oh Lord, Am I Still Single?" prayer, this is actually the "Why, Oh Lord, Have I Made Poor Choices?" prayer. (The two aren't unrelated.) And as you discover why you've done what you've done until now, it's possible you might end up being less single than you are at this moment. But first things first.

There's a lot about ourselves that we don't see . . . until we see it. And I'm convinced that there is fabulous potential for growth and transformation, though getting at it is a little bit counterintuitive. Namely, there's value in noticing some of the bad choices we've made. We can learn to make healthy future choices by examining those past ones, possibly even breaking the old patterns that have kept us stuck.

1. **God, help me to notice the poor choices I've made in the past.** In my case, I chose a good man—albeit a homosexual one—because he was "safe," when my childhood home was not. By definition, he was not the best choice for me, since I'm heterosexual. Ask God to open your eyes to see the choices you've made that haven't served you well.

2. **God, help me to recognize what's driving my choices today.** Ask God to show you how your attractions have been driven by a desire to receive the emotional nutrition you justly deserve but didn't receive. We do this by laying before God the formative adults in our lives, particularly the ones who, in the words of my Uber driver, "gave us the hardest time." Notice their emotional maturity or

immaturity, ability to be emotionally present to you, addictions, self-centeredness, emotional or physical absence, etc. Ask God to open your eyes to your experience of your earliest caregivers. This isn't about blame or faultfinding. It's about becoming aware of what you already *know* in your deep places. It's about recognizing the ways in which you may still be attracted to what you experienced because you're seeking the emotional nutrition you justly deserve.

3. **God, help me make better choices in the future.** When my Love-Yoda Uber driver suggested that single folks need to look for someone "boring," my heart sank. Every time I scroll through a dating app, I am willfully trying to find someone who is *not* boring. But all of my failure leads me to believe that Lo-Yo might be right. So it is with open hands and open hearts that we release our bad instincts and poor choices to the Almighty, asking God to lead us by the Holy Spirit to make better choices.

TEACH ME TO LOVE LIKE YOU LOVE

We were made for love. But love doesn't always have to look like dating a man until it leads to marriage (though I know this particular path is the reason most of us are on dating sites). We probably already have a good idea of what love could look like in a marriage, but what about a man you don't marry? Love also looks like letting a man know the ways that you see the image of God shining through him. Love looks like praying for someone whose profile reveals a lot of pain and brokenness. Love looks like being kind and direct when you need to end a relationship. When I have felt the most despondent and focused on my own wants, needs, and happiness, I have found amazing relief when God has given me the opportunity to care for someone else—especially someone I wasn't interested in dating but who I wanted to befriend. Truly, it's magic. Try it. Whether you are just discovering who someone is, or you're on that third date, or you're letting a man know you don't see the relationship moving forward, pray, asking God, *Teach me to love like you love.*

I'm curious about the prayer that wells up inside *you* when you speak to God about dating or finding a marriage partner. Maybe you've been praying for the man you anticipate meeting, in God's timing. Maybe there's a single word you hold in your heart—like *patience* or *love*—as you do yoga. The One who is present to every moment of your journey is listening.

PRAYER EXERCISE

This week, ask God which of these eight prayers, or a similar one, has your name on it. Set an alarm on your phone to remind you to offer it to God. When you sense God is releasing you to move on, choose a new prayer. Start a conversation with God today.

- Not My Will but Yours
- I'm Lonely
- Send Someone or Take This Desire from Me

- Help Me to See What You See
- Takes My Eyes Off Myself
- Guide My Next Step
- Why, Oh Lord?
- Teach Me to Love Like You Love

BRIEF PHRASES

Some brief phrases that I pray to express my trust in God:

- God, this is yours.
- I am yours.
- I accept your will.
- My relationships are yours.
- Prepare the one who is for me.
- What I consider success is yours.
- What I consider failure is yours.
- I am trusting you.

Be grounded in what is most real as you share your heart with the One who cares.

ACKNOWLEDGMENTS

Because I'm convinced that the deep need of our hearts is to be seen and heard and known and loved, I'm particularly thankful for those with skin on who've embodied that real, gracious, loving presence by being all up in my business.

Greg, you saw something in me, in my writing, that made you say *yes*. And you continue to see what I might do and who I might be. Thank you.

Jenny, you caught the vision for this book baby and I could not have asked for a more skilled, insightful, and supportive labor partner. I appreciate who you've been—as an editor and a friend.

Most recently, I'm grateful for the group of faithful, thoughtful women—both silent and chatty—in our online care group whose name I swore would not have the word *squad* in it when I launched it last year. So SCWOD (Single Christian Women Online Dating), thank you for your loving presence and support. I treasure y'all.

And daily I'm indebted to the women—in North Carolina, Tennessee, and Alaska—who've walked with me on this dating journey: Bekah, Charlene, Cherrie, Emily, Kay, Lisa, Lizbeth, Lola, Susan, Vaneetha, and whoever else I'll be mortified to realize I've forgotten once this is in print. You've shared my joy. You've grieved my losses. You've encouraged me to take risks and you've protected me from harm. Each of you offered me something unique, a gift that only you could give, that I've desperately needed on this journey.

I'm also grateful that the Father of Jesus has been all tangled up in this mess that is my dating life. When new losses trigger old hurts, this faithful God whispers in my ear, "I got you, girl. This is a new opportunity for freedom, and I'm right here. We got this."

For any and all who've seen me, heard me, known me, and loved me as I've traveled this road: *thank you.*

Margot

NOTES

Chapter 2: Hesitations

1. Brené Brown, "The Power of Vulnerability," TEDxHouston, June 2010, https://www.ted.com/talks/brene_brown_on_vulnerability/.
2. Hayley Matthews, "Who Uses Online Dating? 7 Important Statistics," DatingAdvice.com, last updated December 5, 2019, https://www.datingadvice.com/online-dating/who-uses-online-dating.
3. Matthews, "Who Uses Online Dating?"
4. Matthews, "Who Uses Online Dating?"

Chapter 4: Don't Say Nothing

1. Joe Tracy, "How Many Online Dating Sites Are There?" Online Dating Magazine, March 22, 2012, https://www.onlinedatingmagazine.com/faq/howmanyonlinedatingsitesarethere.html.

Chapter 5: Shine

1. *Hitch*, directed by Andy Tennant (Columbia Pictures, 2005), DVD.

Chapter 6: "Say Cheese!"

1. Isabel Thottam, "10 Online Dating Statistics You Should Know," eHarmony, https://www.eharmony.com/online-dating-statistics/.

Chapter 9: Starting Strong

1. *The Sound of Music*, directed by Robert Wise (20th Century Fox, 1965), DVD.
2. C. S. Lewis, *Mere Christianity* (New York: Macmillan, 1952), 128.
3. Sage Lazzaro, "These 12 Emojis Get You the Most Responses on Dating Apps," Observer, April 10, 2017, https://observer.com /2017/04/best-emojis-for-online-dating-app-flirting-clover/.
4. Madeleine Cummings, "People Who Use Many Emojis in Online Dating Profiles Are Perceived as Less Intelligent: MacEwan University Study," *Edmonton Journal*, May 14, 2017, https:// edmontonjournal.com/news/local-news/people-who-use-many -emojis-in-online-dating-profiles-are-perceived-as-lessintelligent -macewan-university-study.

Chapter 10: Let's Talk About Sex, Baby

1. Amber Brooks, "21 Amazing Online Dating Statistics—The Good, Bad & Weird (2019)," DatingAdvice.com, updated October 23, 2019, https://www.datingadvice.com/online-dating /online-dating-statistics.

Chapter 11: What We Bring to Dating from Our Past

1. Henri J. M. Nouwen, *The Inner Voice of Love* (New York: Random House, 1996), 113, 114.

Chapter 14: Attraction

1. Malcolm Gladwell, *Blink* (New York: Little, Brown and Company, 2005), chapter 2.
2. "16 Scary Statistics of Online Dating," Phactual, https://www .phactual.com/16-scary-statistics-of-online-dating/.
3. Deborah Ward, "The Familiarity Principle of Attraction," *Psychology Today*, February 10, 2013, https://www.psychology today.com/us/blog/sense-and-sensitivity/201302/the-familiarity -principle-attraction.
4. Leonard Sturdivant, Relationship Expert.

Chapter 16: Courage

1. Brooks, "21 Amazing Online Dating Statistics."
2. Aaron Smith and Monica Anderson, "5 Facts About Online Dating," Pew Research Center, February 29, 2016, https://internet.psych.wisc.edu/wp-content/uploads/532-Master/532-UnitPages/Unit-06/Smith_Pew_OnlineDating_2016a.pdf.

Chapter 17: Red Flags

1. *Hitch*, Columbia Pictures.
2. Suzanne Degges-White, "Love Bombing: A Narcissist's Secret Weapon," *Psychology Today*, April 13, 2018, https://www.psychologytoday.com/us/blog/lifetime-connections/201804/love-bombing-narcissists-secret-weapon.
3. Degges-White, "Love Bombing."
4. Greg Hodge, "The Ugly Truth of Online Dating: Top 10 Lies Told by Internet Daters," HuffPost, October 10, 2012, https://www.huffpost.com/entry/online-dating-lies_b_1930053.
5. Hayley Matthews, "27 Online Dating Statistics & What They Mean for the Future of Dating," DatingNews.com, June 15, 2018, https://www.datingnews.com/industry-trends/online-dating-statistics-what-they-mean-for-future/.

Chapter 18: Practicing Self-Care While Dating

1. "Race and Attraction, 2009–2014," OKCupid, September 10, 2014, https://theblog.okcupid.com/race-and-attraction-2009-2014-107dcbb4f060.

Chapter 19: Suspicion, Smarts, and Safety

1. "Catfishing: Don't Take the Bait," (infographic), FreeDating.co.uk, https://www.freedating.co.uk/infographics/catfishing-dont-take-the-bait.html.
2. Alyson Shontell, "7 Things Fake Online Dating Profiles Usually Say," Business Insider, May 12, 2013, https://www.businessinsider.com/7-things-fake-online-dating-profiles-usually-say-2013-5.

Chapter 23: Loneliness

1. Nouwen, 47.
2. Nouwen, 47.

Chapter 24: One Happy Ending

1. Thottam, "10 Online Dating Statistics."

Chapter 33: Hope

1. Lois Smith Brady, "The Writer Anne Lamott Gets to the Happily-Ever-After Part," *New York Times*, April 26, 2019, https://www.nytimes.com/2019/04/26/fashion/weddings/the-final-chapters-of-anne-lamotts-life-now-include-a-soul-mate.html.
2. Anne Lamott (@AnneLamott), "Never give up, no matter how things look or how long they take. Don't quit before the miracle," Twitter, April 12, 2019, 9:16 a.m., https://twitter.com/annelamott/status/1116706754362896384.

Resources for the Journey

1. Jen Pollock Michel, *Teach Us to Want: Longing, Ambition and the Life of Faith* (Downers Grove, IL: InterVarsity, 2014), 30.

ABOUT THE AUTHOR

Margot Starbuck is an award-winning, *New York Times* best-selling author, writing teacher, and speaker. She earned a masters of divinity from Princeton Theological Seminary and a bachelor's degree from Westmont College. She lives in Durham, North Carolina, with her three fabulous teenagers, in a community built around friends with disabilities. Learn more at www.MargotStarbuck.com.